Palazzo Te
in Mantua

Gianna Suitner
Chiara Tellini Perina

Palazzo Te
in Mantua

Electa

Translation
Christopher Huw Evans

Cover
Giulio Romano, "Sala dei Giganti,"
detail.

Contents

"Let us go finally, master, to San
Sebastiano, that is to say to the Te,
for perhaps Julio Romano will have
discovered some divine history."

P. Aretino, *Il Marescalco*, act IV, scene 5.

The Prince and the Artist

Chiara Tellini Perina

The construction of the Palazzo Te in Mantua was an artistic event of the first order art, not only in the history of the state ruled by the house of Gonzaga, but also for the whole of northern Italy, to which the influence of Giulio Romano soon spread, bringing to the North what Vasari describes as the "modern manner."

The story of the Palazzo Te is also an outstanding example of a harmony of intent and culture between patron and artist: Federico II Gonzaga, first Marquis then Duke of Mantua, and Giulio Pippi, known as the Roman.

Federico was born in Mantua in the year 1500, to Marchese Francesco, who had defeated the French army of Charles VIII at Fornovo, and to Isabella d'Este, whose name holds an illustrious place in the annals of the Renaissance as an enlightened patron of artists and an enthusiastic collector of antiques and objets d'art.

At the beginning of the sixteenth century the Gonzaga seigniory had already carved out a role of its own as an artistic patron at the highest level. The hospitality of the Mantua court had been extended to artists such as Pisanello, Brunelleschi, Antonio Manetti, Luciano Laurana, Leon Battista Alberti, and Luca Fancelli. From as far back as the time of Gianfrancesco Gonzaga, Mantua could claim to be the cradle of Humanism: Ludovico, who was to become the second Marquis of Mantua (1441-1478), and his brothers were educated at the school run by Vittorino da Feltre, where they were exposed to ancient Greek culture.

In 1459 the humanist pope Pius II Piccolomini requested Mantua to host a council to discuss the organization of a crusade against the Turks. For eight months the city of the Gonzagas was transformed into the seat of the pontifical court, attracting an exceptional number of influential figures from the worlds of politics and culture. It was during the time when the council was being held that Alberti came to the Gonzaga court, bringing a manuscript of Vitruvius with him. During his stay in Mantua he was commissioned by Ludovico Gonzaga to draw up plans for the church of San Sebastiano. That fateful year of 1459 also saw the arrival in Mantua of Andrea Mantegna, who was to hold the undisputed position of master of all the arts at the Gonzaga court throughout the second half of the fifteenth century. In the *Camera picta* of Mantua Castle Mantegna achieved the most extraordinary realization of the principles of perspective to be found in the Po region of Italy, as well as an impassioned evocation of the ancient world. The paintings on the walls of this room included one of the finest representations of a court ever to be painted, with references to the history of the family and political messages that have been the subject of penetrating modern interpretations. The *Camera picta* can fairly be described as a paradigm of family and civil ethics in the Albertian mold.

Isabella d'Este inaugurated a quite different cultural climate. As well as her "Grotto," in which refined collections of marbles, bronzes, musical instruments, and gems were housed, the marchesa's studio contained canvases by Mantegna, Lorenzo Costa, Perugino, and Correggio, which last are in the Louvre today. The paintings by these artists illustrate a theme of neo-Platonic inspiration that was typical of the courtly culture of the time: the triumph of Harmony; the victory of heavenly love, or Anteros, over earthly love, or Eros.

At the beginning of the century Isabella's apartment in the old court of the ducal palace in Mantua had the appearance of a refined, inward-looking microcosm that bore no relation to the city. The enjoyment of poetic inventions—to use one of Isabella's own expressions—was possible, owing to the complex iconological and philosophical references involved, only to a narrow circle of humanists and courtiers.

It was inevitable that Isabella's son Federico, still a young man at the time of his succession in 1519, would find this world of highly erudite images old fashioned, not only because of the severity of the moral code that it expressed, but also because the refined artistic language in which it was couched had now been rendered archaic by Roman and Florentine innovations.

In 1506 Mantegna, who had remained in Mantua almost all this time, died and no one else could assume a role like the one he had played, in either painting or architecture.

8

For around fifteen years a large number of artists passed through the court, and were given prestigious commissions, but not one of them was able to leave such a decisive mark on the city as the great master had done during his years of activity.

It is clear that Federico Gonzaga was determined to find a new talent whom he could entrust not only with promotion of the figurative arts, but also with building up the image of the prince and his state. Unlike Isabella d'Este, Federico wanted to manifest his own authority and the political relations of the state in the form of magnificent buildings and a general renewal of the urban fabric the city had inherited from the Middle Ages and the early Renaissance. Even the decorations had to play their part in this celebration of the family's status.

It is significant that when Federico mounted the throne in 1519, he tried to get Raphael to design the sepulchral monument to his father, Francesco Gonzaga. It was no accident that the young marchese turned to the man who was considered prince of the arts in Rome.

As a young boy Federico had been a hostage of the papal court as a result of complex political maneuvers. During the night between the 7 and 8 of August 1509 Francesco Gonzaga, who had joined the League of Cambrai against Venice, had been captured by the army of the Serenissima at Isola della Scala and sent to Venice as a prisoner. Isabella d'Este, having assumed regency of the state, undertook complicated diplomatic negotiations to obtain her husband's freedom. As a condition of his liberation, the young Federico Gonzaga was sent as a hostage to the papal court.

Thus Federico, as a guest of Pope Julius II, had been able to witness, between 1510 and 1513, the flowering of the arts in Rome. Bramante, Michelangelo, and Raphael were all at work in the city. The young prince was able to admire the completed Belvedere, the beginning of work on the new basilica of St. Peter, the Vatican rooms, and the frescoes on the ceiling of the Sistine chapel. The letters sent to Isabella by Stazio Gadio and other Mantuan correspondents containing news about her son are of great importance. His visits to the rooms in which Raphael was working are indispensable to any evaluation of the understanding that later developed between the prince and his artist.

A no less important influence on him in Rome was the current fervor over archeological discoveries that lay behind new directions in style and a lively surge in collecting. Federico Gonzaga inherited his mother's passion for antiquity and would always maintain contacts with Rome for the purchase and exchange of ancient statues and marbles. His desire to bring to Mantua a Roman artist, imbued with that city's aura and sharing in its cultural atmosphere, takes on the air of a necessary choice, from which a new face for the city of the Gonzaga was to result.

Mantua, described by Vasari after Giulio Romano's interventions as a "new Rome," was to become a bridgehead of the "modern manner" in northern Italy. Mantua's example was to lead to radical changes in artistic language in Emilia, Veneto, and Lombardy, by means of a rapid diffusion of the Roman innovations brought in by Giulio. But let us go back to the story of the artist and his patron.

Titian, Portrait of Giulio Romano, c. 1536. (Formerly) Manila, Marcos Collection.

In 1521 Federico Gonzaga, using Baldassar Castiglione as a go-between, began the negotiations to bring Raphael's most illustrious pupil, Giulio Romano, to Mantua. Giulio Pippi, born in either 1492 or 1499, had served his apprenticeship with Raphael, collaborating on major projects of architecture and painting. He had assisted Raphael in his work on Palazzo Branconio dell'Aquila and on Villa Madama, certainly on the decoration and probably on the architecture as well. Giulio had also collaborated with Raphael on the decoration of the Vatican rooms and loggias, as well as on the Cupid and Psyche cycle at the Farnesina. A large number of movable paintings—of controversial autography—also came out of the collaboration of Raphael, Giulio Romano, and Gianfrancesco Penni.

Works in Rome that are ascribed to Giulio Romano's autonomous activity include the villa of Baldassare Turini on the Janiculum (Villa Lante), Palazzo Stati Maccarani, the restoration of the house at Macello de' Corbi in which the artist was born (now destroyed), and the design of Palazzo Adimari-Salviati.

It was with this important body of work behind him that the artist landed on the banks of the Mincio in 1524. In a letter to Baldassar Castiglione dated 29 August 1524, Federico Gonzaga wrote of his unalloyed esteem for Raphael's pupil and his eagerness "to employ his most noble genius both in painting and in architecture."

Work already under way on Federico's suburban residence of Marmirolo was interrupted so as to permit Giulio to come up with a new design for the existing large group of buildings. The improvement of the villa (destroyed in the eighteenth century) was Giulio's first assignment in Mantua.

What he did at Marmirolo and, from 1526 onward, the Palazzo Te must have met with Federico Gonzaga's approval. On 5 June 1526 Giulio Romano was granted Mantuan citizenship and within a few days he received a house in the Leopardo ward, adjoining the basilica of Sant'Andrea, as a gift from Federico. On 30 August of the same year Giulio Romano was appointed prefect of the Gonzaga buildings and court vicar; on 20 November he was given the post of supervisor of urban streets.

He was held in boundless regard in the city and led a comfortable life: "he lived like a great lord" commented Benvenuto Cellini who visited him in 1528.

The prince's acts of generosity were matched on the artist's part by tireless dedication: Giulio's output was as high as his imagination was unlimited, covering a vast range of artistic creations. To use Vasari's words, Giulio Romano created "a new extravagant manner."

Let us now take a look at Federico Gonzaga's public and private life. In 1518 the prince, just returned from a visit to France where he had stayed from 1515 to 1517, fell passionately in love with Isabella Boschetti, the wife of Francesco Cauzzi Calvisano Gonzaga. In 1523 Federico was appointed captain-general of the Church and of Florence. The events of the years 1530-1532— which saw Federico win the favor of Emperor Charles V, the elevation of Mantua to a duchy, and the marriage of the lord of Mantua to Margherita Paleologo—will be discussed during the course of the description of the decorations of the Palazzo Te, which are closely bound up with these developments.

The increased authority of the prince and of the state of Mantua was reflected in the ardor of Giulio's work. In the ducal palace the Rustica was constructed and the Troia apartment decorated. Giulio Romano worked on the latter in collaboration with Titian. Titian painted a very fine portrait of Giulio (formerly in the Marcos Collection, Manila) in which the artist is depicted displaying a complicated drawing of a building on a central plan. Another of the works Giulio carried out in the palace was the house for Margherita Paleologo.

For the court Giulio Romano prepared designs for tapestries, furnishings and silverware, theatrical scenery and costumes, and a number of temporary decorations.

Giulio provided the city with monumental gates and buildings for public use, such as butcher's and fishmonger's shops, as well as renovating the Customs House. The artist also designed villas in the surrounding countryside and religious buildings such as the abbey church of San Benedetto in Polirone and the Cathedral and bishop's palace in Mantua.

Giulio Romano was also asked to work outside the borders of the Gonzaga state. In Vicenza the artist was invited to solve the problem of the reconstruction of the loggias of the Palazzo della Ragione. On this occasion he may also have drawn up the plans for Palazzo Thiene and the Villa Thiene at Quinto.

In Verona the facade of Palazzo Canossa is tentatively attributed to Giulio. There is no doubt, however, that in 1534 Giulio provided cartoons for the frescoes in the apse of the Verona Cathedral, which were executed by Torbido. Giulio Romano received requests for cartoons for tapestries from the courts of France and Ferrara and from Ferrante Gonzaga, Count of Guastalla and governor of Milan.

In 1540 the Confraternity of the church of the Steccata in Parma commissioned a design representing the *Coronation of the Virgin* from Giulio Romano, to be used for a fresco on the vault of the apse.

Vasari says that, at the time of his visit to Mantua in 1541, he saw in the artist's house plans of all the buildings that had been constructed to his design, not only in Mantua and Rome, but all over Lombardy.

The pupils trained in Giulio's bottega helped to spread their master's ideas throughout the north of Italy. Some of Giulio's designs even made their way across the Alps: the Landshut residence in Bavaria is reminiscent of the Palazzo Te and many of his ideas, taken to France by his talented pupil Francesco Primaticcio, were adopted for the Fontainebleau palace.

For a number of great artists like Palladio, Titian, and Paolo Veronese, the lessons they learned from Giulio were of pivotal importance.

Evidence of Giulio's appeal comes from the admiring comments of contemporaries such as Baldassar Castiglione, Aretino, Benvenuto Cellini, and Vasari. His fame even reached, by roundabout ways, the ears of Shakespeare, who referred to Giulio in *The Winter's Tale* (act V, scene 2) as "that rare Italian master...."

Federico Gonzaga died in 1540. Giulio Romano was destined to survive him by six years. It is exceptional for a partnership between patron and artist to have produced such extraordinary results, changing the appearance not just of a palace but of an entire city. After Federico's death Cardinal Ercole Gonzaga assumed the regency of the state, confirming Giulio Romano in his role. He was given new commissions and completed his own house. The salon of the latter contained representations of the Olympian gods, along with other paintings celebrating antiquity, the Roman world, prosperity, and peace.

In 1546 Giulio received an important commission from Rome: on the death of Antonio da Sangallo the younger, those in charge of the work on St. Peter's decided to entrust Pippi with the responsibility for its construction.

But Giulio procrastinated, partly because of pressure from Cardinal Ercole who wanted to keep him in Mantua. On 1 November 1546 the artist died and was buried in the church of San Barnaba, close to his home.

Cardinal Ercole expressed his sorrow at the loss of the artist to his brother Ferrante Gonzaga in these words: "My grief at the loss of our Giulio Romano is so great that I feel as if I have lost my right hand."

The Location and Chronology of the Palazzo

Gianna Suitner

At its southern limits, the insular structure of the city of Mantua was defined, not by a lake, but by a dike, called the Magistrale, which connected the waters of the Lago Superiore, near Porta Pradella, to those of the Lago Inferiore, near Porta Cerese. Along this line was built, at the end of the fourteenth century, the third ring of walls, completing the medieval city's long process of formation and expansion. Porta Pusterla was constructed in the middle of the southern circle of walls, of secondary importance with respect to the main gates of the city. The city was traversed from north to south by a route that provided an ideal link between the Gonzaga residence of the Ducal Palace and the church of San Sebastiano (Alberti, 1450) and with the palace, also known as San Sebastiano, built toward the end of the fifteenth century.

The opening of Porta Pusterla extended this route, aptly described by Carpeggiani as the "Gonzagas' private axis" beyond the walls and over the dike as far as the island of the Te. This was where the Gonzagas kept their stud farms and stables. But the island of the Te had been used as a place of entertainment ever since the days of Marchese Ludovico: in 1459, during the Diet of Mantua, he took his guests there to watch a female leopard run. In 1480 Marchesa Barbara, Ludovico's widow, wrote that "we keep that place on the The for our pleasure."

In Gabriele Bertazzolo's perspective view of Mantua, printed in 1628, the complex on the island of the Te looks like the result of a comprehensive environmental project that adorns and reinforces the presence of Giulio's building. The latter stands at a tangent to a long tree-lined avenue that leads from the Pusterla gate and bridge onto the vast plain surrounded by the Paiolo (today the area of the Te Brunetti). Among the cultivated fields are gardens and a large maze.

The idea of rebuilding the old Pusterla gate formed part of the same scheme for improving the island. The project, which was never carried out, can clearly be seen in Giulio Romano's designs for a gate (Stockholm, National Museum, 360/1863; Vienna, Albertina, 14203 and 14204). These drawings, which Hartt (1958) regarded as preliminary studies for the Giulia gate, erected to Giulio's

design in 1549, have recently been identified (Tafuri, 1989) as plans for the gate of the Te. The place's island character has been lost today. With the filling in of the Magistrale dike and demolition of the Pusterla gate and the city walls in 1905, the complex of the Te, although surrounded by an area laid out as gardens, has been swallowed up by the recent featureless expansion of the city and squeezed, to the south, by the railway line.

Giulio Romano and Federico II Gonzaga, marquis of Mantua "[...]" went out of the gate of San Bastiano, a crossbow's shot distant, where His Excellence had a place and certain stables, called the T, in the midst of grassland, where he kept the stock of his stallions and mares: and come to this place, the marchese said that he would like, without spoiling the old walls, to set up a little place to which he could go, and withdraw sometimes to draw or to dine out. Giulio, having heard the marchese's desire, looked at the whole place and surveyed the plan of that site, set to work; and making use of the old walls, made in the bigger part the first hall, that one sees today on entering, with the suite of rooms that place it in the middle: and since the place has no living stone nor quarries at hand so as to be able to make ashlars and cut stones, "[...]" he used bricks and fired materials, working them after with stucco; and out of this material he made columns, bases, capitals, cornices, doors, windows, and other works, with beautiful proportions, and in a new and extravagant manner the ornaments of the vaults, with very fine divisions inside, and with richly decorated receptacles: which was the reason that from a humble beginning the marchese resolved to make all that building in the guise of a grand palace."

This is how Vasari (1880, V, 536), on his return from Mantua where he saw Giulio Romano's designs and visited the city in the artist's company, relates the way in which Federico II Gonzaga conceived the idea of turning the stables that his family had owned on the island of the Te since the fifteenth century into a grand palace. As far as we are concerned, Vasari's passage contains two important observations. The first draws attention to the fact that in the

Gabriele Bertazzolo, "Urbis Mantuae descriptio," Mantua 1628.

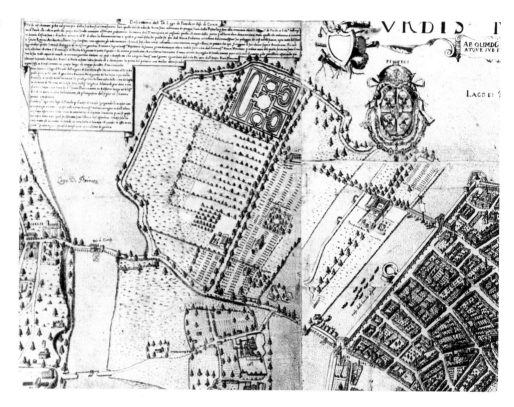

construction of the Palazzo Te, Giulio used to a large extent the structure of the existing Gonzaga stables. The second indicates how the whole complex, starting out "from a humble beginning," was later transformed "in the guise of a grand palace." On the first point, thanks to the arguments put forward by Shearman (1967), recent criticism (*Giulio Romano*, 1989) is unanimous in fully accepting Vasari's account. Archeological investigations carried out during the recent restoration (1987-1989) also suggest that the preexisting structures were laid out on a quadrangular plan, comparable to that of an enclosed courtyard of the Po Valley type (Nicolini, 1984), that is followed fairly closely by the later building. The part of the Gonzaga farm that seems to have conditioned Giulio's design to the greatest extent was the northern block in which the largest hall of the villa is located: the hall known as the "Sala dei Cavalli" (Room of the Horses)

as its decoration consisted of paintings of the prince's favorite horses. Confirmation of this comes from the fragments of fresco decoration, dating from the early years of the sixteenth century, that can still be found above the floors and vaults of the "Camera di Ovidio" (Chamber of Ovid), the "Camera delle Imprese" (Chamber of the Devices), the "Loggia delle Muse" (Loggia of the Muses), and the "Sala di Psiche" (Room of Psyche).

With regard to Vasari's second observation, on the other hand, there is still some doubt as to the accuracy of an initial "humble beginning," transformed by Giulio's "beautiful design" in the "guise of a grand palace." In this case the documentary sources and archeological investigations do not help to clarify whether we are to understand by "humble beginning" an intervention—of restructuring as we would call it today—limited at the start to just one of the blocks of the Gonzaga stables and later extended to the whole complex as part of a broader and more general scheme of design, or that Vasari's comment refers to the transformation of the building wrought by the extraordinary and all-embracing work of decoration.

The fact remains that while the vast *corpus* of documents, recently set in order, relating to Giulio Romano's activity in Mantua (1524-1546) tells us almost everything about the work meetings, the artists, and even the materials used for the decorations of the rooms, it is elusive, imprecise, and incomplete where the phases in the construction of Federico II Gonzaga's villa are concerned. As a result the question remains open of the relationship between the general idea of the project, documented it seems by the drawings in Berlin ("Study for the plan of Palazzo Te," in the *Mantuan Album* of Marten van Heemskerck, II, Berlin, Staatliche Museen) and in Düsseldorf (Kunstmuseum) and the actual stages in its construction.

One of the possible and more reasonable interpretations, based on the collation of Vasari's account with the few indirect documentary facts and a critical interpretation of the architecture, suggests three fairly easily distinguishable stages in the history of the Palazzo Te.

The first of these would coincide with the internal redistribution of spaces in the Gonzaga stables, starting out from the north wing. It seems that while work was being carried out on the restructuring of the interiors, decoration of the rooms was commenced as soon as they were ready. This second stage took up a considerable number of years in the middle of the period dedicated to the construction of the villa (1524/25-1534).

The third phase would have corresponded to the realization of the facades.

Let us try then, as far as possible, to trace a chronology of the interventions and alterations that have given the complex the form in which we see it today.

On the basis of the available documents, work commenced on the Palazzo Te sometime between Giulio's arrival in Mantua (end of November 1524) and February 1526, when Federico II Gonzaga requested materials "to get finished a number of places which we desire to be finished with all promptness" in the "building of ours that we are having made at present on the Te."

In this first phase the rooms on the north side were prepared, the ones located between the "Camera di Ovidio" and the "Sala dei Cavalli" and "Sala di Psiche," and separated by the "Loggia delle Muse," at that time considered the official entrance to the villa.

One fact that allows us to say for certain that work on the spaces in this northern block was complete is the decoration of the *camerone* of Psyche with oil paintings. Work on this cycle, which was completed in the summer of 1528, appears to have already been under way in June 1526.

As for the dates of the work on the other three blocks of the quadrangular complex, we do not know whether it was carried out contemporaneously with the first intervention or followed it in gradual stages. In any case the aforementioned plan of the Palazzo Te in Berlin, thought to be a design sketch (Belluzzi, Forster, 1989), provides confirmation that Giulio had a plan for the general restructuring of all the rooms in mind right from the start. The bills of payment of 1527, relating to the decorations that were nearing completion in the northern block and to the ones that were being carried out in the "Camera dei Candelabri" (Chamber of the Candelabre), in the southern block as well as in the eastern block, prove that between the end of 1526 and the beginning of 1527 work had been extended to the whole of the structure and that it had, although only partially, also involved the areas outside, where for instance the fishponds were under construction. Hence there was a decisive turning point in the work on the villa between 1526 and 1527—a turning point that may have been the result of a new and different interest on the part of Federico in the alterations being made to the Te. In fact up until that time the marchese had been more concerned with his residence at Marmirolo, where work had been going on without a break for nearly a century (it had been begun by Gianfrancesco in 1435) and for which Giulio Romano himself had sent a design from Rome in the March of 1523. It may very well have been in this year that the "humble beginning" to which Vasari refers was superseded by a more ambitious project. A hint of a change in attitude on the part of the marchese can also be detected in the different tone of Federico's letters over these two years. In the letter mentioning the work on the Palazzo Te quoted above, he had made a vague reference to the "building of ours that we are having made at present," while in a subsequent letter of 22 February 1527 he spoke explicitly of the "building of our Palace."

Notwithstanding the undoubtedly broader conception of the intervention, there is no hint in any of the documents from 1527 of the idea or intention of giving an overall design to the facades. Windows and doors were made wherever they were required by the internal distribution of the building and, as is demonstrated by the fragments of decoration discovered on the north side and in the small balcony of the "Sala di Psiche," the outside surfaces of the walls were plastered and decorated with simple geometrical designs. In this connection the landscape painted in 1527 in the "Camera di Ovidio" ("Appartamento delle Metamorfosi" [Apartment of the Metamorphoses], north block) is interesting. The fresco, which depicts the north side of the Palazzo Te overlooking the waters of the canal that surrounded the island, shows the appearance of the facade prior to their redesign. The outline of the villa is sketched in a fairly summary fashion, but it is possible to make out the three arched openings in the middle of the wall, corresponding to the entrance from the side of the "Loggia delle Muse." On the second floor there is a suggestion of an unbroken row of square windows, which must have been those of the mezzanines, although Giulio later interrupted this sequence above the three openings of the entrance. However the painting shows no sign of the pilaster strips that pattern the facade; there is no hint of the rustication, nor of the balcony at the top with its triple dormer window matching the entrance that we can see in the drawings by Andreasi (Kunstmuseum, Düsseldorf) and that was eliminated in the course of the restorations carried out in the eighteenth century.

Right through 1528 activity was intensified in every part of the complex. Work was under way on the ceiling of the "Sala dei Cavalli." The "Sala di Psiche" was being painted, for Federico Gonzaga had asked for the work to be finished so that he could stay there during the winter. The "Camera dei Venti" (Chamber of the Winds) and "Camera delle Aquile" (Chamber of the Eagles) in the east wing "near the fishpond" were being decorated, as was a room in the west block "near the ball court."

We have no direct documentation of the court used for the ball game, a place where Charles V appears to have spent many hours during his first visit to Mantua (March 1530) "playing ball in the Lord's game." Demolished during the nineteenth century, it is referred to in the eighteenth century drawings and plans as *Racchetta* (Racket). This part of the building adjoining the "Sala dei Giganti" (Room of the Giants), was an extension of the east block, and was symmetrical with the volume of the *casetta rustica* (also demolished during the nineteenth century) that stood on the opposite western side adjoining the kitchen area, of which it may have been an annex. These two parts of the complex probably predated Giulio Romano's intervention: in the documents they are always used as references to identify places with no name on which work was being carried out and treated as existing structures. More generally speaking, however, it can be said that the south block, although an occasional reference to the work that was going on there has come down to us, was the section that least interested both Giulio Romano and the marchese himself. This may have been the reason for the incomplete state of the southern loggia and the lack of decorations in many of the rooms in this wing.

In 1528 building work was still being carried out on the mezzanine above the "Camera dei Venti," which was going to be used as Federico II's wardrobe, and on that of the rooms on the second floor of the north wing, above the "Appartamento delle Metamorfosi" (which are now used to house the Acerbi Collection). It was during this same period that construction of the "Appartamento del Giardino Segreto" (Apartment of the Secret Garden) was begun. Work was still being done in 1530 and appears not to have been

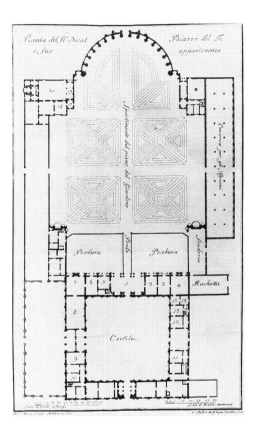

completed until 1534, along with the decorations. From 1529 on the first references to finishing work on the exteriors appear in the documents. It seems that this was started on the western side, where in the summer the fishponds were "enameled" and work commenced on the facade "from where the frieze is made."

During the time which passed between Charles V's first and second visit to Mantua, that is between March 1530 and the fall of 1532, it appears that construction work was interrupted in order to finish off, in a hurried and perfunctory fashion, the decorations in the "Loggia di Davide" (Loggia of David) and the "Sala dei Giganti."

The documents in the archives tell us that it was not until around the end of 1532 and the beginning of 1533 that work commenced in uninterrupted fashion on the facades. Starting with the "Cortile d'Onore," (Court of Honor), the metopes of the trabeation were set in place.

Yet it should be pointed out that in this year Federico Gonzaga's interest in the construction of his palace may have already begun to wane. Numerous notes indicate his renewed interest in the Marmirolo villa where it seems that he stayed for longer and longer periods. This new attitude on the part of the marchese may have something to do with the fact that parts of the Te complex were not completed, or at least turned out differently from the original plans.

One of the annotations by Jacopo Strada (Vienna, Nationalbibliothek, cod. 9039) to the drawings of the Palazzo Te made by Ippolito Andreasi, known as Andreasino, between 1567 and 1568 (Düsseldorf, Kunstmuseum) states that the southern loggia was "not finished nor even enclosed" and that the outer face, overlooking the ball court, was not executed in the same way as the others. The idea that Giulio Romano left some parts unfinished and that the Palazzo Te was never completed was again suggested by Strada in his comment on another of the drawings by Andreasino. According to Jacopo Strada in fact, a plan of the palace, in his possession and drawn by Giulio himself, reveals that the original project envisaged another building of quadrangular shape, similar to the first. This second building, which was intended to house the "services pertaining to the court of a great prince" was to have stood, according to the most recent criticism (Belluzzi, Forster, 1989), on the other side of the fishponds, in the area of the garden.

The last documents connected with Giulio Romano's activity, dating from 1534, are concerned with the decorations and stucco work in the small chambers and in the "Loggia di Davide," and the frescoes still being painted in the "Sala dei Giganti."

From that year on, even though work on the Palazzo Te was never officially halted, activity slowed almost to a complete standstill, while notes began to appear on the need for maintenance work or even restoration (the frescoes in the "Appartamento del Giardino Segreto").

At the end of the sixteenth century the two buildings that stand at the ends of the fishponds were built, perhaps by Gabriele Bertazzolo. In the one on the right, looking toward the facade of the "Loggia di Davide," was located the hydraulic machinery that operated the fountains and kept the water circulating in the ponds. This water was taken from the canal (now filled in) that surrounded the island. Over the same period the southern loggia of the Court of Honor, which, as was mentioned above, was never completed, was partially enclosed and turned into a room.

At the beginning of the seventeenth century the Grotto was constructed in the end room of the Secret Garden. In 1651 Nicolò Sebregondi, the designer of a lodge (never built) that was to have stood in the middle of the palace's largest garden, enclosed the area not yet bounded by the garden with the Exedra and built the Fruit Houses along the southern side.

But the most significant alterations were made during the restorations carried out at the end of the eighteenth century at the behest of the Austrian administration and under the guidance of the Veronese architect Paolo Pozzo. All the floors inside were replaced, the position of a number of doors shifted ("Loggia di Davide," "Sala dei Giganti," "Sala dei Cavalli"), and changes made to the colors of the stucco decorations ("Sala degli Stucchi" [Room of the Stuccoes]). In the Court of Honor the graduation of colors was eliminated and the diversity and irregularity of the rustic work smoothed out, making the outlines more rigid and regular.

In general the facades took on the appearance they have today, with the demolition of the balconies at the top and the dormer windows, originally set in the middle of the fronts at the same point as the loggias beneath.

Lastly the second row of balconies on the facade overlooking the garden was demolished and the structure of the "Loggia di Davide" topped by a triangular tympanum. A second campaign of restoration, entrusted to Giovanni Antonio Antolini between 1805 and 1806, attempted to check the deterioration of the rooms and gardens. But the long periods of abandonment, and the frequent and improper use of the rooms (as stables and military storehouses) have left a deep mark on the structure. It has also suffered greatly from the loss of its original relationship with the surroundings and from having been swallowed up by an extraneous urban structure, the suburban development that has grown up around it.

The Architecture

Gianna Suitner

At first sight the complex of the Te looks like a work of exemplary simplicity and clarity. The regularity of layout of the square, compact, and sturdy structure is apparent even from the outside. The square plan governs the entire development of its spaces. In the two facades to the north and the west the different spacing of the pilaster strips divides up the surfaces in relation to the function of the corresponding rooms. Thus the closely spaced pattern at the ends of the facades, which matches the distribution of the apartments around the corners of the building, gradually thins out toward the center, where the entrances to the building are located.

On the *northern facade*, facing the city, a triple archway, framed by two pilaster strips, leads into a portico. Behind this, further into the building, stands the "Loggia delle Muse." On the *western facade*, the space taken up by the entrance has only a single archway. However the greater importance of the wall at that point is emphasized by the framing of the entranceway by the motif of a double pilaster strip separated by a recess; it is a pattern that echoes the design of the corners.

In the design of the facades, both outside and inside, the use of the classical order on a gigantic scale is one of those elements that lends itself to interpretation on two levels. On the level of detail, in fact, the squaring of the surface produced by the tall and massive pilaster strips emphasizes the spatial relationship between the hall on the ground floor and the mezzanine above. In some cases the latter space is used for additional rooms ("Appartamento di Ovidio"), while in others ("Appartamento dell'Imperatore" [Apartment of the Emperor]) it is equipped as a service area (*stufetta* or bathroom, dressing room, cabinet). From a more general point of view, however, the tall pilaster strips, running between a rusticated basement in deep relief and an uninterrupted cornice decorated with triglyphs and metopes, look like an explicit attempt to reduce the overall mass of the building to a single story. The architectural elements or citations from the classical repertory, typical of the architectural language used by Giulio Romano, demand a continuous and attentive effort of interpretation, owing to the different indications or suggestions that result, for instance, from the transition from the particular to the general.

The clarity of the spatial layout on the one hand, and the two planes on which it can be interpreted on the other, make the Palazzo Te into one of most difficult architectural works of the early Cinquecento, but also one of the most fascinating. As one ventures deeper into analysis of the structure, one discovers, for example, that the use of classical motifs takes on a very precise significance in Giulio's language that goes far beyond mere citation. The elements of the classical repertory (rustication, pilaster strips, metopes, triglyphs, trabeations), while retaining their intrinsic value, are used in a new and wholly original way. A perfect example of this is the way that the careful calculation of the projections of the pilaster strips and the degree to which the cornice is set back not only recalls the idea of a trabeation but also creates the impression of a load-bearing structure.

The strong three-dimensional effect of the lower rustication links the bed of the windows to the base of the pilaster strips. In this way both are made part of the socle of the building. The vibration of the upper rustication, slight and increasing gradually till it reaches its maximum projection at the keystone of the window, and the change in the texture of the wall surface between ground floor and mezzanine serve to create an architecture of illusion in which the tradional values of load-bearing structure and superstructure are turned on their head. The sequence of broad and bulky pilaster strips, set on the outside edge of the bed on which the building stands, takes on the role of a structural framework that supports a long, slightly recessed cornice, used as trabeation. The wall on the contrary, which is actually load-bearing and looks heavy because of the rustication, loses its structural consistency to take on the appearance of a screen stretched between pillars as a mere enclosure or curtain.

The references to classical architecture, which we shall see to be determinant in the design of the internal facades, appear vague

and elusive here. The resemblances—between the bed of the building, with a flight of steps running up it on the western side, and the crepidoma of a Greek temple, between the cornice, with the devices of the Gonzaga carved in the square spaces of the metopes, and the trabeation of a building from the classical era, or between the triforium of the entrance loggia and the supporting arch of a Roman gate—are not sufficient to obscure the image of the traditional Po Valley enclosed courtyard that determines the plan of the building.

Once past the *western loggia*, the building's entrance hall, the simplicity and clarity of the layout, already perceptible from the outside, emerge even more strongly. From the center of the *Court of Honor* the planimetric design is visible in its entirety, laid out around the perimeter of a large square of roughly forty-five meters on a side. The four apartments that make up the palace of Federico II Gonzaga, and whose traditional names derive from the theme of the decorations of their rooms, are set around the corners of the central courtyard and delimited by the open loggias in the middle of the facades.

Thus if we start from the entrance hall and move in a clockwise direction, we find: the "Appartamento di Ovidio" or "Appartamento delle Metamorfosi," located between the western loggia (entrance) and the "Loggia delle Muse"; the "Appartamento di Psiche," located between the "Loggia delle Muse" and the "Loggia di Davide" the "Appartamento dell'Imperatore" or "Appartamento delle Aquile," located between the "Loggia di Davide" and the southern loggia; and the "Appartamento per la familia et ufitiali" (Apartment for the Family and Officers), located between the southern loggia and the western one (entrance).

A distinctive feature of the distribution of spaces in the palace is the consequential way that each apartment is linked to the loggia before it in a repetitive pattern running right round the central square. But the most original element is the loggia itself. In the general plan, this space ensures that the four apartments are kept strictly separate and distinct. In particular, it is the node through which all possible routes in the building must pass. The loggia establishes a continuity in the route around the perimeter, permitting a sort of internal relationship between the apartments, but it also represents the only link between the rooms and the exterior, whether inside the courtyard or outside the palace.

It has now been demonstrated (Belluzzi, Capezzali, 1976; *Giulio Romano*, 1989) that the peculiar features of the layout of the Palazzo Te can be traced back to the model of the Roman *domus*, which Giulio Romano had studied in an edition of Vitruvius illustrated by Fra Giocondo. However the exceptions that Giulio introduced into his reworking of Vitruvius's model, in order to adapt the ancient style of living to the requirements and conditions laid down by Federico Gonzaga, make the parallel less immediately obvious. The Palazzo Te, for instance, consists of a single, large quadrangular block, while we know that the Roman house was made up of two parts whose respective centers were the *atrium* and the *peristilium*, separated by a room open on side like a loggia, the *tablinum*.

If, however, we consider the possibility, only recently come to light, that the Palazzo Te, which was never completed, is only the first nucleus of a much larger complex, divided into two blocks set on opposite sides of the fishponds, then the parallels with the *domus* become closer and clearer. For one thing, this would explain Giulio Romano's insistence that the Te complex should look as if it had only one story, both from outside and from the internal courtyard. Just as in the Roman house, use of the upper floor is limited to a few rooms created out of the space below the roof, recognizable from the outside by the windows of the mezzanines that have not been walled up.

In fact each of the four apartments has a group of small rooms on the second floor, decorated in an intimate and private manner. These service rooms are excluded from the public route through the building that is located on the ground floor and do not play a part in the calculated study of the visual relationships established among the elements of the apartment: between the door of a room and the opposite wall with the fireplace, or among the doors of a group of

rooms, arranged in a line to form a long perspective. These upper rooms have no spatial relationship except with the room beneath, through small and well-concealed staircases set in the spaces between two successive rooms, or located in the service corridors behind the rooms.

In the four groups of usable rooms on the second floor, the following have been identified: a wardrobe, now occupied by the Egyptian Collection of Giuseppe Acerbi, above the "Appartamento delle Metamorfosi"; Federico II Gonzaga's wardrobe, above the "Camera delle Aquile"; service rooms for the servants, above the western apartment where the kitchen is located, and which now house the Gonzaga Collection of dies, coins, and medals (fourteenth-eighteenth century); and another wardrobe, in the southern wing, above the "Appartamento dell'Imperatore." The most interesting room in this last group is the *stufetta*, or bathroom. Separated from what has been identified as the cabinet and preceded by a dressing room, this small rectangular room is concluded by a niche decorated with very fine stuccowork. From the typological viewpoint this room is a curiosity that has two illustrious precedents in the *stufetta* in the Vatican palaces designed by Raphael for Cardinal Bibiena and in Clement VII's bathroom in Castel Sant'Angelo, attributed to Giulio Romano himself.

Returning to our examination of the complex as a whole, the spatial element of the loggia, one of the most unusual features of Giulio's design, also has a close parallel in the model of the Roman house. The western loggia with the entrance and the "Loggia di Davide" opposite are equivalent to the *vestibulum* and the *tablinum*; the northern loggia, or "Loggia delle Muse," and the southern one, although shifted to an anomalous position at the center of the building, are the equivalent of the two wings that normally flanked the *tablinum*.

In Giulio's distribution of the spaces the four openings of the loggias seem to have the same weight and value. Their architectural designs, although with two different, symmetrically matching forms, reveal his intention of emphasizing the functional distinc-

24 tions of the ancient model. Consistently with the layout, the device used to bring out functional differences or to emphasize nodal points of the spatial articulation is citation from the classical repertory of forms. But in Giulio's language citations—widely used as we shall see—seem not to derive directly from a reading of the classical texts, but to have passed through the filter of the modifications made by Raphael, Baldassare Peruzzi, or the members of the Sangallo family, to mention just a few names. And it is interesting to note how, if we move from the vestibule used as the entrance to the palace through the Court of Honor to the "Loggia di Davide," the sequence of sources that can be identified follows, step by step, the course taken by Giulio in Rome along with the other artists in Raphael's circle.

The division of the space in the vestibule, based on the projection of a Serlian motif, finds precise parallels in Raphael's designs for Villa Madama and in the atrium of Palazzo Farnese, designed by Sangallo the younger, both in Rome. The Court of Honor, based on the pattern of the Tuscan court without columns, and the "Loggia di Davide," turned into a large hall opening onto the waters of the fishponds by the elimination of the eastern wall, also hark back to similar solutions adopted in the villa designed by Raphael.

As well as the citation, another of the specific and dominant characteristics of Giulio's art can be identified in the vestibule: elements designed and executed with extreme care and refinement are set in a dialectical relationship with other, roughly worked elements. Examples of this are to be found in the ceiling, where the connecting parts, made up of large rusticated ashlars, are inserted into the refined pattern of square lacunars (rectilinear in the lateral sections) and octagonal lacunars (in the

barrel-vaulted central section). But there is also the contrast between the shafts of the columns, swollen and rough as if they had just been hewn out of a block of marble, and the capitals and bases, finished and polished with extreme care. Or again the design of the walls, patterned with heavy pilaster strips and semicircular niches finished in stucco.

The "poetics of opposites," as Tafuri has defined (1989) this particular aspect of Giulio's creativity, becomes still more apparent in the *Court of Honor*.

The internal facades that surround the square area of the court are patterned with a grid that resembles the one on the external facades in the regular sequence of elements of the classical order. But the vertical structure that divides up the wall into square sections of rustication, in which are inserted windows, mock windows, or niches, is more bulky, more polished, and more luminous too here on the inside, owing to the use of half columns instead of pilaster strips.

Today, unfortunately, these contrasts, which must have originally been given even greater emphasis by the colors of the now vanished fresco decorations, are attenuated by the sort of homogenization that the recent restoration work has conferred on the different architectural elements. However if we continue with the patient observation of details, it becomes apparent that the device of placing discordant elements side by side to create astounding effects of illusion is extended to cover every inch of the walls. Even the tiniest detail is a reflection of this approach, apparently without any particular logic but with an extraordinary exercise of the imagination. It suffices to notice, for instance, how the continual variations in the grain or thickness or cut of the rusticated ashlars reduce the structural quality of the walls almost to nothing, even though the mass of the masonry as a whole gives an impression of weight and power. The same contradiction can be seen, for example, in the windows on the west side. The tympanum-shaped canopies are mounted on polished corbels. The large rusticated ashlars that, arranged in a sunburst, are intended to suggest the idea of a curved architrave, are also polished. The large, roughly hewn, rusticated keystone, however, is pushed upward so as to force apart the pitches of the canopy.

26

The open canopy and the broken architrave, both recurrent motifs in Giulio Romano's architecture, are like colossuses with feet of clay. They create a powerful impression owing to their size, but lose all structural value.

More generally speaking, then, on the facades of the Court of Honor, just as we have noted on the external facades, the annulment of the load-bearing capacity of the walls emphasizes a structural grid that is not real, but whose apparent massiveness seems to have been entrusted with the role of supporting the huge roof of the palace.

Among these contrasts and illusions, one highly unusual element is worthy of separate mention: the *slipped triglyph*. Giulio Romano used it only for the internal facades of the Palazzo Te. The long and uninterrupted cornice that links together the four faces of the Court of Honor is certainly intended to be seen as a trabeation, and as

such it alternates the motif of the metopes with that of the triglyphs. On the western and eastern facades, however, the triglyph at the center of the intercolumniation is made to slip downwards, creating the impression of a break, or a subsidence, in the trabeation at that point. It is clear that by this device the structural element loses its intrinsic value in order to restore to the wall the structural role that had been denied it by the graduation of the surfaces.

The overall effect is a subtle and complicated interweaving of shifts and illusions that leaves us amazed and dumbfounded, for we find ourselves unable to identify the exact role of any part of the structure.

The originality of the design, which lends itself to a wide variety of interpretations, has at times been seen as a caprice, at others as transgression or playful discord, or even as irony or self-mockery (Carpeggiani, Tellini Perina, 1987; Tafuri, 1989). Yet it should

*Foreshortenings of the vestibule
of the western entrance.*

be remembered that motifs like the broken architrave, the slipped stone, the ruined wall with rusticated ashlars, or the rusticated ashlars rotated and corroded until they take on an undulating profile (which we see in the curtain walls of the western mezzanines) are all details that can be found in Giuliano da Sangallo's drawings of ancient buildings (Barberini Codex, ff. 4, 25v., 26, 29v., 30).

That particular style of ancient culture in which curiosities were combined with hints of ruin—"excesses of bloody wounds of extraordinary interpretative license" (Borsi, 1985)—was in common use among the artists of Raphael's circle and cannot have been unfamiliar to Giulio Romano.

So motifs like the slipped triglyph, broken trabeation, cut architrave (used again by Giulio in the portico of the Rustica in the Ducal Palace), and open tympana can also be seen and interpreted as Pippi's fondness for ruins, used to undeniably illusionistic ends.

Another feature worthy of particular attention is represented by the *reliefs of the metopes* with their carvings of the *devices* of the Gonzagas. As is well-known, the *device* represents an important aspect of court culture owing to its ties with philosophy and symbolic literature and to its connection with the decorative theme of the grotesque and the art of commemoration. Thus the device proposes lines of conduct or programs for living, expressed by means of mottos and figures. It is founded on the combination of word and image, bringing to mind Horace's maxim *ut pictura poesis*.

From the figurative point of view, the device is made up of a symbolic design (body) and a motto (soul), both of which are vital to understanding its meaning. They allude to the virtues, usually moral, of the family or person for whom it is designed. This decorative theme, a favorite of the Gonzaga since the end of the fourteenth century, was used in the Palazzo Te both as a decoration in relief (in the metopes of the outer and inner facades, in the lacunars of the ceiling in the "Sala dei Cavalli," and on the fireplaces) and as a pictorial decoration (for example in the "Camera delle Imprese," or Chamber of Devices, and in the Secret Garden).

The literary sources behind many of the

30

twenty-four devices that are used in different areas of the house have been identified some time ago and their emblematic significance laid bare. This is true of the majority of the devices carved in the metopes of the courtyard and the outer facades. They include the famous ones of the salamander and Mount Olympus (Signorini, 1985); the one of the dog, which appears many times in the castle of San Giorgio; the ancient one of the fawn and the lure, which appears for perhaps the first time in the frieze of the so-called "Corridoio del Passerino" (Corridor of the Passerine) in the Palazzo del Capitano of the Ducal Palace, dating from the last quarter of the fourteenth century (Bazzotti, 1986; Suitner, 1989); and those of the noseband, the sun, the turtledove, the crucible, the glove, and the bills of fortune (Praz, 1981; Signorini, 1985). Many of the others are probably more recent in origin and may be connected with the figure of

Federico II Gonzaga or of his mother Isabella, but although they have been reported and discussed (Bazzotti, 1989), they are still awaiting an explanation.

All these elements serve to lend a certain degree of uniformity and homogeneity to the four facades. Yet careful examination shows that the designs and subdivisions of each section of the facades are determined and conditioned by the pattern of internal distribution. The intervals between the half columns that delimit the sections of wall and that frame the windows, for example, are not constant. Neither does the subdivision of the trabeations into metopes and triglyphs conform to a regular pattern. They vary in size and number in order to fit the gaps between pilaster strips on the outer facades and the gaps between half columns on the inner ones. The anomaly is especially obvious in the design of the outer northwest corner.

32

We can amuse ourselves by carrying on the search for Giulio's errors or exceptions, but the case of the north facade overlooking the court can serve as an example for all.

The displacement of the "Loggia delle Muse" with respect to the median axis that runs across the courtyard is certainly determined by the size of the "Sala dei Cavalli," just as the same room forces Giulio to use a smaller, and from the compositional viewpoint not very satisfactory, window at the point where this block meets up with the western one. The difference not only in size but also in shape of this corner opening looks like an improvised solution, adopted by the architect without too much concern, indeed in a rather offhand manner.

It is clear therefore that, by the time Giulio set to work on the facades, between 1532 and 1553, the constraints imposed by the preexisting structures—whether those of the old Gonzaga stables or of the rooms whose forms had already been determined and many of which were already decorated—had a decisive influence on the whole layout and composition of the facades.

Giulio Romano encountered still greater difficulties in the design of the eastern face of the "Loggia di Davide." The deviations, irregularities, anomalies, and exceptions can only be explained by a preponderance of concern for the view from the inside looking out. The spatial nodes that determine the design of the eastern facade, looking onto the fishponds, are: to the north, the "Sala di Psiche," hinge of the northeast corner and the center of Federico II Gonzaga's private suite of rooms; to the south, the "Sala dei Giganti," hinge of the southeast corner and center of the "Appartamento dell'Imperatore" or "Appartamento delle Aquile"; and in the middle, the "Loggia di Davide." The latter, which represents the meeting point of the apartments on each side of it, is laid out not so much as an area of passage but rather, in a clear echo of the *tablinum* of the Roman *domus*, as an open but sheltered space in which people could spend time.

Comparing the three spaces, we can see how in the two rooms the internal space was constructed, articulated, or disarticulated by the effects of the pictorial decoration—

effects that alter the shape of the vaults, break up the walls, and swallow up the real openings, making them part of the illusion. As a result the layout of the decoration in itself excludes the possibility of a manipulation of the architectural structures to fit with the design of the facade.

In the loggia, on the other hand, the freedom from conditions imposed by existing spatial considerations allowed Giulio to come up with an intrinsically autonomous architectural solution.

On the side of the Court of Honor, the rectangular space, oriented along the north-south longitudinal axis, is sealed off by a screen of walling pierced solely by the doorway. The doorway is aligned in perspective with the entrance vestibule of the palace on one side (the western) and with the bridge that spans the fishponds, the large garden, and the exedra that are located beyond the "Loggia di Davide" on the other (eastern side). Three wide arches are set in the front

of the loggia, set on a tetrastyle structure of columns linked by a slab carved to resemble trabeation. An alternation of archways and architraved connections, running both along the loggia and across it, forms a complicated echo of the Serlian motif that is used in the vestibule of the entrance. But here the architectural order is embellished with a refined and detailed stucco decoration in relief.

Emerging from the splendid and luminous "Loggia di Davide" and crossing the bridge over the fishponds, we can look back at the whole span of the *eastern facade*. The three sections referred to above are clearly distinguishable.

This side of the building presents us with a clear demonstration of the design method used by Giulio Romano in the organization of the facades. He followed a process that was based on successive decisions, both in time and space, taken as each problem or

34

node to be resolved presented itself. An anti-architectural process, if by architecture is meant that global vision whose product is the synthesis of the relationship and correspondence between the internal space and the design of the exterior. In the front of the "Loggia di Davide," in fact, the unitary appearance of the central block, corresponding to the space of the loggia, is contrasted, in the lateral sections, by partial solutions to which the generalized use of the Serlian motif does not lend coherence of composition. To realize this it is enough to note how the fixed points of the faces of the two wings are the positions and dimensions of the arches that frame the windows of the rooms behind: the "Sala di Psiche," "Sala dei Venti," and "Camera delle Aquile" on one side, and the "Sala dei Giganti," "Camera dell'Imperatore," and "Sala egli Stucchi" on the other. The intermediate parts, consisting of the straight connections between arches, are of different lengths since they have to absorb and conceal the sections of wall that separate the chambers. Even the supports of the Serlian motifs, chosen to frame the balcony from the inside of the room behind, are different. Note, for example, the group of coupled pilaster strips with a semicircular recess in the middle at the end of the north facade, as well as the Serlian motif supported on one side by a small column and on the other by a pair of pilaster strips. Thus it can be seen that while each Serlian motif has what might be called its own internal coherence, the same cannot be said of the composition of the facade as a whole. These shifts in dimension and mixed Serlian motifs—in other words this lack of homogeneity—have been seen as Giulio's personal and original elaboration of "halting rhythms," or as an expression of his "liking for the unexpected" or "for the irregular," or even "as an attempt to create a dynamic equilibrium in which the disconnectedness is the result of deliberate asymmetries" (Tafuri, 1989).

But even these undoubted discords and asymmetries, like the motif of the slipped triglyph in the Court of Honor, are open to a variety of interpretations.

In fact if we reconsider the hypothesis—suggested by Jacopo Strada's annotation to

38

*Facade of the Loggia di Davide facing
the garden.*

Following pages:
*Foreshortening of the eastern side
with the fishponds.*

39

the drawings of the Palazzo Te (Belluzzi, Forster, 1989)—of a second quadrangular building, to be set symmetrically opposite on the far side of the fishponds, then we may have another key to the interpretation of the eastern facade. The other building "[...] that made a perfect square in which there were all the services pertaining to the court of a great prince [...]," separated from the first only by the short bridge that emerges from the "Loggia di Davide," would have meant that the facade could only have been viewed from very close up and above all from a single point. In which case the "halting rhythms" of the lateral sections of the facade would not have had much relevance. The only important thing would have been the long perspective that extends between the "Loggia di Davide" and the western entrance on the far side of the Court of Honor.

If we go along with the hypothesis of a doubling of the quadrangular layout, the "Loggia di Davide" would have formed the dominant pole of perspective for anyone following the route the other way round.

Further evidence in support of this interpretation seems to come from the fact that the facade of the loggia was decorated with frescoes (in 1532) by Fermo da Caravaggio, depicting victories, barbarians, and prisoners. Thus the loggia would have been the intermediary node of the larger complex divided into two identical and symmetrical nuclei, of which the one we can see today was the only one built.

Lastly, it remains to be said that the present facade is considerably different in appearance from the form it was given by Giulio Romano. An idea of the original design, which has not been altered in the lower areas or in the lateral sections of the facade, can be gathered from the drawings made from 1567 onward by Ippolito Andreasi for the Mantuan antiquary Jacopo Strada (Düsseldorf, Kunstmuseum). Above the loggias at the sides, looking onto the waters of the fishponds, ran a second row of small loggias that linked up with the central volume of the "Loggia di Davide." The facade was surmounted by a continuous balcony, identical

to the one on all the other facades, whose subdivisions echoed the pattern of the part below. The belvedere and upper loggias were eliminated at the end of the eighteenth century by the Veronese architect Paolo Pozzo, during the restoration work carried out on behalf of the Austrian administration. The triangular tympanum that crowns the "Loggia di Davide" was also inserted at this time, perhaps in an attempt to bestow on the facade the order and rigor of composition that, from a strictly neoclassical viewpoint, were missing from Giulio's design.

Today the situation of the *external areas* of the Palazzo Te is profoundly different from the way in which Giulio Romano could have imagined or intended it. This is not just because of the failure to realize some parts of the complex or the loss of the fountains that were a vital feature of the garden, but largely the result of the long and inexorable process of transformation that commenced almost immediately after the deaths of Duke Federico II (1540) and his architect (1546).

Along the southern edge of the large walled garden runs the block of the fruit houses (conservatories for citrus plants). This was added on around the middle of the seventeenth century by Nicolò Sebregondi, and involved demolishing a section of the southern end of Giulio's complex. The volume that closes off this side of the garden was used as a house for the gardener (and now contains the offices of the body responsible for the upkeep of the Palazzo Te) and formed a *pendant* to the small building that stands at the opposite end.

This last is the core of the "Appartamento del Giardino Segreto," also known as the "Appartamento della Grotta" (Apartment of the Grotto) after the grotto that was constructed there around the turn of the six-

*Detail of the Loggia di Davide
from the garden.*

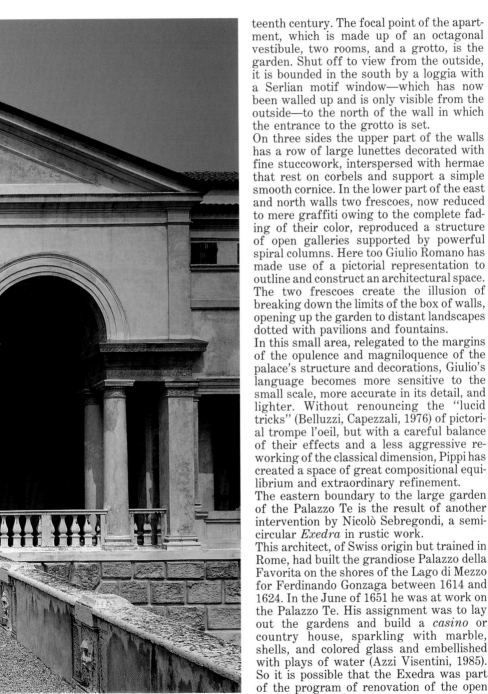

teenth century. The focal point of the apartment, which is made up of an octagonal vestibule, two rooms, and a grotto, is the garden. Shut off to view from the outside, it is bounded in the south by a loggia with a Serlian motif window—which has now been walled up and is only visible from the outside—to the north of the wall in which the entrance to the grotto is set.

On three sides the upper part of the walls has a row of large lunettes decorated with fine stuccowork, interspersed with hermae that rest on corbels and support a simple smooth cornice. In the lower part of the east and north walls two frescoes, now reduced to mere graffiti owing to the complete fading of their color, reproduced a structure of open galleries supported by powerful spiral columns. Here too Giulio Romano has made use of a pictorial representation to outline and construct an architectural space. The two frescoes create the illusion of breaking down the limits of the box of walls, opening up the garden to distant landscapes dotted with pavilions and fountains.

In this small area, relegated to the margins of the opulence and magniloquence of the palace's structure and decorations, Giulio's language becomes more sensitive to the small scale, more accurate in its detail, and lighter. Without renouncing the "lucid tricks" (Belluzzi, Capezzali, 1976) of pictorial trompe l'oeil, but with a careful balance of their effects and a less aggressive reworking of the classical dimension, Pippi has created a space of great compositional equilibrium and extraordinary refinement.

The eastern boundary to the large garden of the Palazzo Te is the result of another intervention by Nicolò Sebregondi, a semicircular *Exedra* in rustic work.

This architect, of Swiss origin but trained in Rome, had built the grandiose Palazzo della Favorita on the shores of the Lago di Mezzo for Ferdinando Gonzaga between 1614 and 1624. In the June of 1651 he was at work on the Palazzo Te. His assignment was to lay out the gardens and build a *casino* or country house, sparkling with marble, shells, and colored glass and embellished with plays of water (Azzi Visentini, 1985). So it is possible that the Exedra was part of the program of renovation of the open

spaces of the Te and that it was built in the years around 1651.

There is no clue in the documentation as to how Giulio Romano might have intended to close the perimeter of the eastern area. But in the fresco of *Arcturus* in the "Sala dei Venti" there is the outline of an exedra, arranged in a semicircle around a pool. The structure appears to be pierced by a sequence of Serlian motifs set on tetrastyle groups of columns and surmounted by a terrace. This motif, which finds a parallel in the court designed by Baldassare Peruzzi (1524) in Palazzo Fusconi-Pichini in Rome (Bruschi, 1986; Tafuri, 1989) and which influenced Giovan Battista Bertani in his layout of the Castello square (c. 1550) in the Ducal Palace of Mantua, was used by Giulio Romano in the "Loggia di Davide."

It is possible then that Sebregondi's Exedra is based on a plan that was originally part of Giulio's project, and to which Federico Gonzaga's architect gave a baroque formal solution.

Finally, heading back through the garden toward the palace, one comes across a small building adjoining the right end of the "Loggia di Davide." Now used as a *bookstore*, it originally housed the hydraulic machinery used to operate the fountains and to keep water circulating through the fishponds. This water was drawn from the canal that surrounded the island on which the Palazzo Te used to stand.

The Decorations

Chiara Tellini Perina

There are a number of keys to the interpretation of the decorations of the Palazzo Te. Of fundamental importance is philological interpretation of the documents and bills of payment that concern the construction and its decoration. These documents have been published as a result of the commendable researches carried out by C. D'Arco, P. Carpi, F. Hartt, and E. Verheyen and of the formidable work on the archives undertaken in preparation for the exhibition devoted to Giulio Romano that was staged in Mantua in 1989.

"The work was brought promptly to its end" was Vasari's comment on the Palazzo Te in the second edition (1568) of the *Lives*. Vasari's account is in keeping with the evidence provided by the chronological span of the payments, which covers the period 1526-1535. The coherent sequence of these payments testifies to the organizational skills of Giulio and the industriousness of his collaborators.

A stylistic comparison between the paintings and stucco decorations as they were realized and the preparatory designs, which form a quite extraordinary *corpus*, is another indispensable premise. It is from this kind of investigation that we gain our knowledge of Giulio Romano's method of working. Borrowing the practice from his teacher Raphael, he placed himself at the head of a complex and well-organized team of collaborators, coming from different regions of Italy, to whom he entrusted the execution of his own ideas, the realization of his own brilliant inventions.

Responsible for the project, Giulio availed himself of the help, for specific areas of specialization, of Gian Francesco Penni (who had been a fellow student in Raphael's bottega in Rome), of Benedetto Pagni da Pescia (also brought from Rome), and of Rinaldo Mantovano, Luca da Faenza known as Figurino, Girolamo da Treviso, Girolamo da Pontremoli, Fermo Ghisoni da Caravaggio, Anselmo Guazzi, and Agostino da Mozzanega, painters specializing in figures and grotesques. The stucco workers included Andrea and Biagio de' Conti and Giovan Battista Mantovano. A certain amount of mystery surrounds the participation of Primaticcio, who was active at the Palazzo Te

until 1531, but only as a stuccoworker. Later on, in France, he was to come up with brilliant elaborations of many of Pippi's ideas in the decoration of Fontainebleau castle.

Another key to understanding the interiors of the Palazzo Te lies in the iconological interpretation of the various decorative representations, which are closely bound up with the function of the villa, the personality of its owner, the history and politics of the state of Mantua, and the ideas of the learned humanists whose active collaboration Giulio sought in the selection of figurative themes. In the interpretation of the grand decorative scheme, attention has to be paid to more subtle but no less influential factors, such as the decoding of devices, the fondness of court circles for self-representation, and the enthusiasm for the revival of classical culture.

Nor should we forget stylistic interpretation, which will show Giulio to be the man who brought the "modern manner" to Mantua, and elsewhere, and who was able to give concreteness and vitality to tales of antiquity with his bizarre inventions, sensual use of material, and feeling for nature.

The earliest documents relating to the Palazzo Te date from 1526 and concern the purchase of materials and classical statues. The first intervention was in the north block ("Sala di Psiche"), on which work was probably carried out from 1526 to 1528. The orders for payment of 1527 concern the rooms on the north side, part of the east side and a few rooms on the south side, such as the one known as the "Camera dei Candelabri." Thus it appears that the decoration was not carried out in separate blocks, since the program of decoration had already been extended to cover the entire square of the court by 1527.

Appartamento delle Metamorfosi

Coming in through the western entrance, the first apartment one encounters is that of the Metamorphoses, comprising the "Camera di Ovidio," "Camera delle Imprese," and "Camera del Sole" (Chamber of the Sun), which is referred to in documents from 1527 and 1528. These are payments in favor

48

49

of Agostino da Mozzanega and Anselmo Guazzi, specialists in small grotesque scenes, and of the stuccoworker Andrea de' Conti.

There is no evidence in the documents for the widespread belief that the rooms of the Metamorphoses were the private apartment of Federico's lover, Isabella Boschetti. However one cannot help noticing the prevalence of decorative themes extolling eroticism and the delights of poetry and music.

Camera di Ovidio

The first room is known as the "Camera di Ovidio," since Ovid's *Metamorphoses*, which were extraordinarily popular in the sixteenth century, form the literary source for the frieze. This frieze is set above another simulating marble inlays. The subjects taken from Ovid, depicted on a dark ground in the manner of the third Pompeiian style, allude to love and fertility: *Apollo and Pan's Dispute with Minerva, Dionysius in a State of Drunkenness,* and *Venus, a Satyr and Maenads* on the eastern wall; *Orpheus in the Underworld* and the *Tor-ment of Marsyas* on the southern wall; the *Judgment of Paris, Bacchus and Ariadne,* and *Dancing Nymphs and Musicians* on the western wall. The "Fables of Ovid"—as the antiquary Jacopo Strada calls them in his sixteenth century description of the building—alternate with small landscapes, painted in summary fashion.

The painted panel in the north wall is of particular interest, as it depicts the Palazzo Te while under construction, in the state it must have been in in 1527: one can see the three arches of the north loggia, but the attic, pilaster strips, and rustication are all lacking.

The wooden ceiling is made up of painted coffers. Agostino da Mozzanega (payment of 1 August 1527) and Anselmo Guazzi were paid for the painting of the ceiling, the figures, and the landscapes. On 8 February 1528 Andrea de' Conti received payment for the execution of the stuccos of the fireplace. Constructed out of red Verona marble, the fireplace bears an inscription with the initials of Federico: F.G.II.M.M.V. (Federico Gonzaga II Marchio Mantuae V.).

50

Camera delle Imprese

The decoration of the "Camera delle Imprese" consists of a frieze imitating marble inlays, underneath a fascia with grotesque decorations in which corbels are inserted. On these rest putti with their arms spread to hold medallions bearing the Gonzaga coat of arms and devices, surrounded by exuberant decorations of leaves and plants. Some of the devices (Olympus, dog, turtledove, glove) allude to fidelity in politics and in love, while others (salamander, Cupid between two trees) are of an amorous nature.

The wooden ceiling is level with painted coffers. The fireplace is inscribed with the initials of Federico (F. II. M. M. V.) and bears the device of the salamander with the motto "Quod huic deest me torquet" (What this lacks torments me). As Paolo Giovio asserts in the *Dialogo delle Imprese militari et amorose* (Lyons, 1574), "this Lizard has many properties, and among them it has one very rare one worthy of wonder among the infinite and marvelous effects of nature; and this is, that he does not go into rut, as does every other animal. Whence the Lord Federigo of Mantua took a very witty device; which was the lizard with the motto, QUOD HUIC DEEST ME TORQUET. And this was the love of his woman, which tormented him; of which love that animal had none."

The device of the salamander, rich in allusions to Federico Gonzaga's sensual temperament, can be taken as emblematic of the iconographic program of the first phase of the palace's decoration.

The heraldic theme of the "Camera delle Imprese" can be found in other Gonzaga residences of the late fifteenth and sixteenth century. However the exuberance of the polychrome frieze in this room of the Palazzo Te marks a decisive move away from the more austere and strictly monochrome stamp of Mantegna, which characterized the rule of Isabella and Francesco Gonzaga.

The frescoed parts of the decoration were executed by two painters from Giulio's team who specialized in small scenes and plant decorations: Anselmo Guazzi and Agostino da Mozzanega.

Camera del Sole

In the late eighteenth century the walls of

Loggia delle Muse, detail of the ceiling.   Sala dei Cavalli.

52 the "Camera del Sole" were decorated with copies of Giulio's stuccos and ancient reliefs, but it is the design of the vault of this room that was extraordinarily innovative—and destined to exert an influence on a European scale (Primaticcio was to use this idea in the gallery of Ulysses at Fontainebleau, just as the motif of the foreshortened view of horses was to influence the young Caravaggio in his decoration of the dressing-room in the Ludovisi—formerly del Monte—villa in Rome). The vault, shaped like a ship's hull turned upside down, is decorated with a pattern of stucco lozenges, studded with figures taken from coins and ancient medals: these include a Pegasus from one of Federico II Gonzaga's coins. At the center is set a panel representing, in a dim light that gives emphasis to the powerful masses, the chariots of the setting sun and the rising moon, suggesting an ideal heavenly parabola. Here Giulio Romano, who was already famous among his contemporaries for the boldness of his foreshortening of perspective, shows that he had given much thought to the example set by Mantegna in the *Camera picta* of Mantua Castle.

There are no documents relating to the "Camera del Sole." It has been suggested that Primaticcio worked on this room. However more recent criticism tends toward the belief that Primaticcio's only contribution to the Palazzo Te was as a stuccoworker. The date of the room's decoration is around 1527, and its style is connected with that of the "Sala di Psiche."

Loggia delle Muse
The north loggia, which links the "Appartamento delle Metamorphosi" to the "Appartamento di Psiche," is devoted to the Muses: the decoration alludes to music and poetry, which were part of the "honest idleness" that motivated the construction and molded the decoration of the palace.

In the lunette set above the entrance to the "Camera del Sole" Apollo is depicted, with mask, pen, and book, holding a flute with seven pipes out of which runs Hippocrene, the spring sacred to the Muses that was made to flow from the rocks of the Helicon by a blow from the hoof of the horse Pegasus, who is represented behind the figure of Apollo.

At the entrance to the "Sala dei Cavalli" can be seen the Muse Urania (also identified as the nymph Castalia or the nymph of Mantua Amymone) standing near a spring, with the head of Virgil and an Apollo. On the basis of stylistic comparison, the two lunettes have been attributed to Rinaldo Mantovano. The walls of the loggia are painted with large landscapes (their state of preservation is too poor for them to be made out clearly) against which are set scenes from the myth of Orpheus and Eurydice, which can be interpreted with the aid of the drawings (Düsseldorf, Kunstmuseum) made by Ippolito Andreasi for the antiquary Jacopo Strada. We will have occasion to refer again to these accurate drawings reproducing the facades and interior decorations of the Palazzo Te. They were commissioned by the antiquary Jacopo Strada, along with those of the "Appartamento di Troia" in the Ducal Palace, during a visit to Mantua in 1567. The original idea can be traced back to Strada's patron, Hans Jacob Fugger, acting on behalf of Duke Albert V of Bavaria. Probably Strada wanted to publish a selection of ancient monuments and contemporary works of art. The drawings are accompanied by a number of annotations ("Ordine come vanno li dissegni del Palazzo del Ti fuori di Mantua," Vienna, Nationalbibliothek) that provide useful information about the condition of the rooms and the decorations. Andreasi's drawings constitute an invaluable testimony to the state of the building in the sixteenth century, prior to the later alterations.

The decoration of the barrel vault of the "Loggia delle Muse" is again a glorification of poetry: elegant stucco figures representing the Muses appear against a complex checkerboard of spaces. The association of the Muses with panels painted with grotesques, containing hieroglyphics of Egyptian inspiration, is an unusual one.

The hermetic culture of the hieroglyphics during the Renaissance was based on Francesco Colonna's *Hypnerotomachia Poliphili* (1499) and the 1505 edition of Horapollo's *Hieroglyphica*. Saving for another time a discussion of Francesco Colonna's text, to which other paintings in the Palazzo Te

54

refer, let us take a look at this erudite source, the *Hieroglyphica*. The book, apparently written by an Egyptian author of the second or fourth century A.D., who may be fictitious, and supposedly translated from the Egyptian into Greek, was discovered by the Florentine priest Cristoforo de' Buondelmonti on the island of Andros in 1419. The book was devoted to a description of the enigmatic hieroglyphics, which were thought to represent ideas rather than letters and sounds, an expression of the secret wisdom guarded by the Egyptian priests.

Learned circles—and evidence for this comes from both Marsilio Ficino and Leon Battista Alberti, who had described the hieroglyphics as the domain of "expert men"—showed a great deal of interest in this discovery.

Ideographic script had also influenced the figurative arts. Pinturicchio in the Borgia rooms of the Vatican and Andrea Mantegna in the *Triumphs of Caesar*, which were originally located in the palace of San Sebastiano in Mantua, not far from the site of the Te, had already made use of this enigmatic script that only the initiated could decipher. It is significant that Giulio Romano used this type of ornament, with its wealth of esoteric messages, in the private residence of his patron, access to which was permitted to men of letters, humanists, and courtiers: it served to indicate a cultured level of enjoyment, not open to the common herd.

Sala dei Cavalli

From the "Loggia delle Muse" one enters the "Sala dei Cavalli," devoted to lauding the steeds that were raised in the stud-farms of the Te and which were much in demand at all the courts of Europe.

Among the manuscripts in the possession of the Gonzagas was *Dell'infermità dei cavalli* ("On the Sickness of Horses," now in the Fondazione D'Arco, Mantua), a fifteenth century work by Zanino Ottolengo, veterinarian to Ludovico II and Federico I Gonzaga. The codex of the *Palii gonzageschi* (Venice, private collection), dating from around 1512 and the work of Silvestro da Lucca, is illustrated with thirty-four miniatures depicting the same number of horses from the Gonzaga stables which had won

races in various Italian cities.

The fact that the names of four horses are also to be found in the "Sala dei Cavalli" of the Palazzo Te—Battaglia, Dario, Morel favorito, and Glorioso—is proof that they are portraits of actual horses, the pride of Federico II Gonzaga's stables. There was also a room dedicated to horses in the villa (now destroyed) at Marmirolo and another room (1536) with this name in the "Appartamento di Troia" in the Ducal Palace of Mantua, further evidence of the Gonzaga's fascination with this theme.

The Room of the Horses in the Palazzo Te was a large hall, and was used for entertainments and receptions. Almost all of Giulio's pupils collaborated—from 1527 to 1528—on its decoration: Rinaldo, Pagni, Fermo da Caravaggio, Girolamo da Pontremoli, Luca da Faenza, Anselmo Guazzi, and Agostino da Mozzanega.

It is possible to distinguish between their work. Rinaldo was responsible for the figures of Jupiter, Juno, Venus, and, among the *Labors of Hercules, Hercules and Antaeus* and *Hercules and the Nemean Lion*.

To Giulio himself is attributed *Hercules and Deianeira*; to Pagni *Hercules and Cerberus* and *Hercules and the Hydra*. The landscapes are attributed to Anselmo Guazzi and Agostino da Mozzanega. The frieze with putti, masks, and foliage is thought to be the work of Fermo Ghisoni. The horses appear to have been painted by Giulio Romano himself.

The ceiling, divided up into panels by twisted ribs, is the work of the carver Gasparo Amigoni, interpreting an idea of Giulio's. The coffers of the ceiling and other spaces contain Federico's devices of the salamander with the motto "Quod huic deest me torquet" and of Mount Olympus.

The device of Mount Olympus, which frequently recurs in the decorations of the palace, also appears on the seals, coins, and medals of Federico Gonzaga. It consists of a mountain with a path winding round it in a spiral, which may be surmounted by an altar with the motto FIDES-OLIMPOS. In a letter dated 3 May 1524 the marchese invited Baldassar Castiglione to have this device set on panels of dressed leather. The device is also mentioned in the imperial patent of

55

Sala di Amore e Psiche, Psyche Sleeping in the Valley of Cupid.

Sala di Amore e Psiche, Psyche Sees Cupid.
Sala di Amore e Psiche, Nymph.

60

8 April 1530 by which Charles V bestowed the title of duke on the Gonzaga.

The floor, which mirrors the geometric pattern of the ceiling, is the result of the restorations carried out in the late eighteenth century by Paolo Pozzo. A hefty rusticated fireplace dominates the south side of the room. The high wainscotting of the walls must have been lined with painted leather.

Giulio Romano, inspired by the examples of Roman palaces, and the "Salone delle Prospettive" in the Farnesina in particular, had the walls painted to represent an architectural structure with Corinthian pillars. Between the pillars are false niches with monochrome paintings of Olympian divinities set in them like statues: Vulcan, above the fireplace, is the *faber* god who rules over horses; Jupiter and Juno correspond to the lord and lady; Mars and Venus preside over war and peace. Above each of the four windows is set a bust, painted in monochrome, in the classical style. Framed inside illusory windows, against a background of landscapes with low horizons, the horses themselves are portrayed with an extraordinary monumentality.

Above the horses are set mock bas-reliefs that imitate the bronze in which the *Labors of Hercules* are represented: a theme, taken from antiquity and associated during the Renaissance with the celebration of heroic figures, that rhetorically glorifies the patron Federico Gonzaga as a new Hercules. Not only did Giulio Romano mix up interior and exterior, pictorial and architectonic space, but he also played tricks with the materials: he imitated marble and bronze, painted mock panels of veined marble between the pillars, and finally returned to the quivering vitality of the horses. The latter were celebrated by Torquato Tasso in verses that praised the verisimilitude of the paintings ("Sovra la camera dei cavalli del Signor Duca di Mantua".)

In the frieze set between ceiling and trabeation, putti play amidst the gaily colored

foliage that is embellished with golden highlights. The putti amuse themselves with masks that sometimes appear to be falling or sticking out: in this way the effect of the architectural framework is negated, in a playful and ironic manner, as the original connection that linked the decoration of the friezes to the areas of transition between wall and ceiling is broken. Once again Giulio surprises us by the use of one of those "liberties" typical of his language.

Sala di Psiche

The central space in this initial phase of the decoration of the palace was the "Sala di Psiche," intended to be used for banquets and memorable for the fact that Emperor Charles V once dined there.

The work on it was carried out by Giulio himself, who wished to give his prince a demonstration of his own painting skills, and by Gianfrancesco Penni, Pagni, Rinaldo Mantovano, Luca da Faenza, and Fermo da Caravaggio, named in payments made from 1527 to 1528, although it has been suggested that work on the design of the room commenced in 1526.

The decorations were originally supplemented by a "panel of red leather with gilded columns." A statue of Venus by Jacopo Sansovino stood in the middle, "so real and alive that it filled with lust the thoughts of anyone who gazed upon it" as Pietro Aretino commented.

All this serves to confirm, leaving aside any more moralistic interpretation, Federico Gonzaga's fondness for explicitly erotic and sensual works of art. It should not be forgotten that the lord of Mantua was to order from Correggio the *Leda* (now in the Berlin Museums) and the *Danae* (now in Rome, at the Galleria Borghese) as gifts for Emperor Charles V.

In the frieze on the walls, on a gold ground, runs the inscription that explains the function of the room: "FEDERICUS GONZAGA II MAR(chio) + V S(anctae) R(omanae) E(cclesiae) ET REIP(ublicae) FLOR(entinae) CAPI-

62

TANEUS GENERALIS HONESTO OCIO POST LABO-
RES AS REPARANDUM VIRT(utem) QUIETI CON-
STRUI MANDAVIT.''
The decoration is divided into three parts:
inserted into the wooden ceiling, and supported on corbels carved in the shape of
acanthus leaves, is a structure in sections,
painted in oil on stucco applied to a lattice
of reeds.
The *Marriage of Cupid and Psyche* is depicted in the central section, with a daring
use of foreshortening that suggests the
influence of the oculus in Mantegna's *Camera picta* in the Ducal Palace.
It is not unlikely that Giulio Romano was also
aware of the parallel experiments with bird's
eye views being conducted by Correggio in
Parma and that he was influenced, in the
strong contrast between light and shade, by
the firework displays and theatrical produc-
tions so commonly staged at the courts.
Around the central compartment are set the
first scenes of the myth, taken from Apuleius's *Metamorphoses*. The beauty of Psyche, who lives in a royal palace with her two
sisters, arouses the envy of Venus, who
decides to punish her: Psyche is to fall in love
with the most worthless man in the world
and for this purpose is left on the top of a
mountain. From there she is carried by
Zephyrus to a valley filled with flowers
where the princess falls asleep. On waken-
ing, Psyche finds herself in a marvelous
palace where a banquet has been prepared,
but nobody appears. In the darkness the
husband for whom she is destined appears,
unseen, and warns Psyche that if she yields
to the temptation of trying to see him, she
will lose him forever. Spurred on by the
malignant insinuations of her sisters, Psyche disobeys the command and approaches
the bed with a lamp and a razor: fascinated
by Cupid's beauty, she draws near and lets
fall a drop of boiling oil, awakening him and
causing him to vanish.
This part of the story is depicted in nine
panels of the ceiling, in a labyrinthine sequence that is again to be found in the

lunettes on the walls, where the story of how Psyche wins Cupid back is illustrated. Ceres and Juno show compassion for the young woman, but do not dare help her for fear of offending Venus. The enraged goddess sends Mercury to capture her. The princess, seized by Habit, is given over to Anguish and Sorrow.

Psyche has to face four ordeals: to pick out seeds from a heap (in which task she is aided by ants); to collect a flock of wool from the shining fleece of certain sheep (in which she is assisted by a reed); to draw water from the river Styx; and finally to bring back from the Underworld a jar containing the beauty of Proserpine.

Psyche, failing to follow the instructions of Proserpine, opens the jar. The jar gives off a malevolent drowsiness that makes the girl fall asleep. Cupid finds and wakes Psyche who, by the intervention of Jupiter, is transported to Heaven where she is made immortal.

The labyrinthine course followed by the episodes painted in the octagons, semi-octagons, and lunettes is a metaphor of the spiritual path that, passing through the perils and trials of initiation, leads to the divine vision.

On earth, a joyful wedding feast is celebrated on the island of Cythera, illustrated on two adjoining walls of the room: a rustic feast or banquet of satyrs on the west wall, a noble scene on the south one. The two scenes present the same subject but make use of different elements of representation. In the *Rustic Banquet* a satyr drinks wine from a goblet and the Horae scatter flowers on the table. One of the three Horae, in the middle, indicates the arrival of Mercury, messenger of the gods. Numerous children are represented as a symbol of good wishes. At the top, above the pergola of myrtle, a plant sacred to Venus, we can see figures of musicians: a Negro satyr with a flute, a female figure with cymbals, and another with a drum to which jingle-bells are attached.

64

66

In the next view of the sky, cupids play with a lizard, tormenting the cold creature with the torch of amorous passion. A putto hands an ink pot to another to complete the inscription "Quod huic deest me tor(quet)" on the scroll.

In the scene of the *Noble Banquet* the following figures can be recognized: from left to right, Vulcan, Apollo seated and crowned with flowers, receiving a cup, Dionysius naked and crowned with ivy, holding a cup and the thyrsus, Silenus, Ceres, and Juno. Above, amidst the clouds, a winged figure playing the horn can be identified as Zephyrus.

The last part of the scene is taken up by the newly-married couple, lying on a golden bed and clasping Voluptuousness, the daughter that will be born from their union. Lying on the ground is a dog, symbol of fidelity. Ceres, wreathed with ears of corn, pours water, a symbol of fertility, on Cupid's hand, while Juno, who presides over births, holds the basin. In the background a group of satyrs can be seen, preparing to sacrifice a goat in front of the effigy of Dionysius.

Opposite the divine banquet on the south walls, the north wall represents the loves of the gods: *Mars and Venus Bathing, Bacchus and Ariadne*, and *Venus, Mars, and Adonis*. The scene of *Mars and Venus Bathing* is set in a cave. Cupid and another winged figure divest Mars of his arms, which lie on the ground. Little cupids are intent on the bath of the goddess, for whom they have set a phial of perfumes on the edge of the tub.

Above the window is depicted the group of *Bacchus and Ariadne*, emblems of orgiastic drunkenness and erotic excitement.

The background to the next scene is a niche covered by a pergola laden with bunches of grapes. In the semicircular space, decorated with statues of men and women, is set a fountain, whose basin, supported by putti, is surmounted by a male figure pouring water from an urn.

The protagonists of the story—which as we shall see has a highly refined literary source—are Venus and Mars, who pursues Adonis with an unsheathed sword. Blood spurts from the goddess's right foot, pricked by a rose, and stains the petals of the flower.

On the east wall, opposite the scene of the satyrs, are depicted the bestial loves: *Zeus and Olympia*, *Polyphemus with Acis and Galatea*, and *Pasiphaë and the Bull*.

Olympia, the future mother of Alexander the Great, was seduced by Jupiter, who presented himself in the guise of a serpent. King Philip, who had dared to look through a crack in the door to observe the scene, lost his eye on that occasion, as Plutarch recounts in his life of Alexander.

The source for the episode of Polyphemus is Ovid's *Metamorphoses*. The famous Cyclops Polyphemus had fallen in love with Galatea, to whom he had promised two bear cubs as a gift. A bear can be seen in the picture, in a cavity in a rock on the left of the Cyclops. But Galatea loved Acis, a love that he returned. The Cyclops, surprising the two lovers, hurled a rock at Acis, who was transformed into a river.

The myth of Pasiphaë is also based on Ovid's *Metamorphoses*. The scene in the "Sala di Psiche" represents Daedalus with a hammer in his hand inviting Pasiphaë to enter the false cow in which she will be able to mate with the bull.

The literary source for the episodes with Mars and Venus as their protagonists is Colonna's *Hypnerotomachia Poliphili*. On the island of Aphrodite, Polya and Polyphilus are watching Venus at her bath, when Mars arrives. Polya and Polyphilus go into a copse, in the middle of which they find a sarcophagus with marble reliefs carved to represent an event that occurred in that place: Venus had taken a bath in the middle of a pergola of roses and had run with bare feet to help Adonis, who was being pursued by Mars. The goddess had pricked her foot on the thorn of a rose, which was stained red by Venus's blood; on every anniversary of the death of Adonis, the white roses would turn red.

The literary sources are extremely refined: Apuleius's fable, originating in the mythical and mystical Orient, was known through Beroaldo's commentary, which appeared in Bologna in 1500. It had already been represented by Raphael, with the assistance of Giulio himself, at the Farnesina in Rome. The *Hypnerotomachia Poliphili*, an allegorical romance imbued with an atmosphere of esotericism that had been published in Venice in 1499, had long been used as a source of images for Renaissance painting. Mario Equicola and Paolo Giovio may have provided the inspiration for the iconographic program of the rooms in the Palazzo Te.

The story of Cupid and Psyche has been seen as an allegory of Federico Gonzaga's love life: Psyche suggests the figure of Isabella Boschetti, the lover of Federico Gonzaga, who is represented by Cupid, while Venus can be interpreted as Isabella d'Este, Federico's mother, who obstructed her son's love affair.

In this room Giulio Romano enriched his genius for composition with a very lively mix of erudite and antiquarian citations, references to the culture of the day (to stage design as well as literature), subtle ironies, and liberties.

Mention has already been made of the influence of Mantegna's *Camera picta* on the artist. In both the structure of the vault and the arrangement of the banquets on two adjacent walls, one can detect an echo of the narrative organization of Mantegna's room. In the octagons, semi-octagons, and vaulting cells of the ceiling a nocturnal atmosphere holds sway, with the artist playing daring tricks with perspective. In his *Osservazioni nella Pittura* (Venice, 1580), Cristoforo Sorte wrote that Giulio "abounded in many very fine inventions, in matters of Painting as well as of Architecture, and concerning the perspectives of planes and foreshortenings."

We can detect an ironic side to Giulio's language in the way that he often introduced facetious and amusing elements into the serious subjects of mythology. On the northern wall, where the trial of the flock of wool stolen from the sheep's fleece is depicted, water pours from every part of the anthropomorphic figure of the river, includ-

68

ing the genitals. This liquid, deliberately ambiguous in nature, appears to overflow into the section underneath, where Mars and Venus are represented bathing in a rocky cave.

Adonis fleeing from Mars is depicted on the same wall: the young man, with naked buttocks, appears to be slipping through an emergency exit, painted like a side-scene, a typical scenic device.

On the opposite wall—the southern one where the *Noble Banquet* is painted—one can see the same theatrical device in the episode of the old woman engaged in conversation with Vulcan while in the act of entering a dark room.

In connection with his interest in temporary decorations and theatrical scenery, it is recorded that in 1530, on the occasion of Emperor Charles V's visit to Mantua, "by order of the Duke, Giulio made many beautiful sets of arches, scenes for plays, and many other things in the invention of which

Giulio had no equal [...]" (Vasari).

New celebrations and performances were staged for Charles V's second visit, in 1532: in November Bibbiena's *Calandra* was put on and the decoration of the scenes entrusted to Giulio Romano.

It is worth pointing out another of Giulio's ironic comments in the representation of the *Rustic Banquet* on the western wall: a river god is depicted on the left, pouring water from a vase and playing with a swan: can this be anything but a malicious reversal of the myth of Leda?

The most daring representation in the room is the one in which Jupiter seduces Olympia. However this is not just an erotic scene, but also a comic one. It should be recalled that, while he was still living in Rome, Giulio had produced a series of sixteen drawings, which he entitled *Manners*, of amorous couplings. The drawings were engraved by Marcantonio Raimondi and accompanied by the same number of licentious sonnets

Sala di Amore e Psiche, Mars and Venus.

Sala di Amore e Psiche, Mars, Venus and Adonis.

*Sala di Amore e Psiche, Jupiter Seduces
Olympia.*

GONZAGA II

by Aretino. The work caused a great scandal in papal Rome.

In the scene representing Jupiter's seduction of Olympia, an improper—and therefore comical in the sense of a "witty remark"—use is made of Jupiter's lightning bolt that, seized by the eagle, drills the eye of the jealous king of Macedonia as he spies on the couple.

This genial manner of recounting the adventures of the gods on earth, with affable appearances and ludicrous modes of behavior, seems to anticipate the mock-heroic vein of Pellegrino Tibaldi in the scenes of Ulysses in the Palazzo Poggi in Bologna.

Another effect typical of Giulio Romano's language is the jump in scale: on the eastern wall of the room — note that this scene is the first to be seen by anyone entering from the "Sala dei Cavalli"—the swollen figure of Polyphemus with his exaggeratedly large club and his pan-pipe seems completely out of proportion to the tiny and elegant fireplace above which it is set.

In the *varietas* of Giulio Romano's language one also encounters refined and erudite citations from reliefs, coins, and classic gems. The group around Apollo in the scene of the *Noble Banquet* is a derivation of the famous Augustan Gem. In the detail of the *klin'e* on which rest Psyche and Cupid in the same scene, we can see the Ouroboros, that is the serpent that bites its own tail, an alchemical symbol of the unity of opposites and of the eternal becoming of nature.

The same southern wall contains other images of extraordinary charm: the landscape to the left and right of the table and the superb display of precious objects. In the section of landscape to the left, representing the procession of triumph over the Indians led by Bacchus, we see a number of exotic personages, a lion, a giraffe, a monkey, and a camel.

Alongside the table there is also an elephant, which harks back to one of Giulio's Roman memories. From 1514 to 1516 the elephant Annone was present in Rome, a gift from the

74

Sala di Amore e Psiche, Landscape.

king of Portugal to Leo X. It caused aston-
ishment among artists as well as ordinary
people. Raphael drew and painted its epitaph
and elephants turn up frequently in the
works of Giulio Romano, especially in the
cartoons for the series of tapestries dedicated to the stories of Scipio.

The central part of the southern wall is
taken up by the dresser with its display of
precious objects: vases, plates, and ampho-
rae which remind us that Giulio had designed silverware and household objects for
the court of Mantua. Unfortunately, all that
survives today of these unusual objects is
a number of drawings.

As far as the division of labor is concerned,
the payments and stylistic comparisons suggest the following. Many sections of the
ceiling can be attributed directly to Giulio
Romano, for example *Psyche and Her Sisters* and *The Marriage*. Giulio's hand can
also be detected in the figure of Mercury

above Polyphemus, in that of Cupid in the
scene in which Venus is angry with Cupid,
in the scene of Psyche at the Styx, and in
the river god above the scene of *Venus and
Mars Bathing*. Giulio was also responsible
for the figures of Charon and the Furies in
the scene of Psyche and Proserpine, the
figure of Mars in the scene of *Mars and
Venus Bathing*, and the figure of Polyphemus.

The high pictorial quality and freshness of
color suggest Giulio Romano's hand in the
banquet, on which the artist was assisted by
Rinaldo Mantovano and Pagni. Giulio did not
make such an extensive contribution to any
other room in the palace, given his own
greater degree of skill and mastery. Many
details show signs of his Roman training:
echoes of Michelangelo can be seen in the
powerful figure of Polyphemus and in that
of Mars at his bath, which recalls the figure
of Adam on the ceiling of the Sistine chapel.
There are also continual iconographic and

stylistic references to the decoration of the Farnesina.

Camera dei Venti

The adjoining room is known as the "Camera dei Venti": work on its pictorial and stucco decorations was carried out from 1527 to 1528. Andrea de' Conti and Nicolò da Milano were responsible for the stuccos, Rinaldo Mantovano, Girolamo da Treviso, Anselmo Guazzi, Agostino da Mozzanega, and Benedetto Pagni for the frescoed parts. The decoration is devoted to a favorite theme of Renaissance culture, astrology. This is indicated by the inscription "Distat enim quae sydera te excipiant," taken from one of Juvenal's satires, written on the door that leads into the adjoining room known as the "Camera delle Aquile."

The works *Astronomica* by the Augustan poet Manilius and *Matheseos libri VIII* by Firmico Materno (fourth century A.D.) have been identified as the sources for the complex iconographic program that has human activities deriving from the rising and setting of particular constellations, ruled by a sign of the zodiac.

At the center of the vault there are three gilded stucco reliefs, representing the Gonzaga device of Mount Olympus, Vulcan, and Vesta. Around them are arranged another ten reliefs in gilded stucco, depicting the same number of divinities. Janus represents January; a satyr represents February, dedicated to the Lupercalia; Mars symbolizes March and Venus April; Maia accompanied by Mercury symbolizes May; Juno symbolizes June. July, August, September, and October are represented by four emperors: Julius Caesar, Augustus, Tiberius, and Commodus or Domitian. The representations of November and December are scenes of putti driving poles into the ground and picking olives. Toward the sides of the room are painted the months of the year, alternating with the signs of the zodiac modeled in gilded stucco. The vaulting cells contain, again in gilded stucco, the masks of the Winds, set above sixteen tondi in which are painted, in fresco, the effects of the astral influences, which may be driven by the winds of fortune.

The zodiacal sign of Aries, under the aspect

77

Camera dei Venti, detail with the fireplace.

of the constellation of the Ship and the Dolphin, imparts particular aptitudes for navigation and swimming, symbolized by the representation of the ship and of swimmers; under the aspect of the constellation of the Goat, it imparts aptitudes for stock-raising and playing the zampogna, a kind of bagpipes, as well as an inclination toward amorous passions, as is indicated by the scene of the pastoral dance. Taurus, in the constellation of the Pleiades, is symbolized by a gladiatorial combat. People born under Gemini, in the constellation of the Hare, will be fast runners, as is suggested by the representation of Hippomenes and Atalanta.

The sign of Cancer, in conjunction with the constellation of Mars, imparts skill in hunting and fishing, as indicated by the scene of men fishing with nets. Those born under the sign of Leo, in relation to the constellation of the Dog Star, will face wild animals without fear, as can be seen in the tondo depicting a struggle between men and beasts. The scene with young people weaving garlands in a garden refers to the sign of Virgo, in the constellation of the Crown, which bestows a love for flowers and gardens. The archers shooting ducks along with fishermen with tridents are connected with the sign of Libra, in the constellation of Sagitta or the Arrow, which imparts a propensity for this kind of occupation.

Those born under Scorpio, in conjunction with the constellation of the Altar, will be priests, or, in conjunction with the constellation of the Centaur, adept at driving coaches, as represented by the two tondi depicting a sacrifice and a horse-drawn coach respectively. The influence of Sagittarius, in conjunction with the setting constellation of Arcturus, will lead people to commit grave crimes punished by imprisonment, as indicated by the tondo depicting a prison. Sagittarius in relation to Arcturus also imparts the propensity to become guardians of royal buildings, as illustrated by the tondo depicting a palace. Those born under Capricorn, in relation to the constellation of Serpentarius or Ophiucus, will be snake charmers, as can be seen in the tondo representing a vendor of theriac, an antidote against snakebite. The scene of Triumph, related to the sign of Aquarius, in the constellation of Aquila, alludes to the warlike virtues typical of those born under this sign. The scene representing the catching of a sea monster, linked to the sign of Pisces, in the constellation of Belua, symbolizes the skill at fishing that is imparted by this sign.

The program for the decoration of this room was probably drawn up by the Neapolitan astrologer Luca Gaurico, who had links with the court of Mantua. Several of the representations may be directly connected with the palace and its owners. Scorpio, which imparts skill in the raising of horses, alludes to the Gonzaga's passion for these animals. Hunting, much loved by the Gonzaga, is represented in the scenes relating to Cancer, Libra, and Pisces. Taurus and Aquarius allude to Federico's skill at arms, Sagittarius to the Gonzaga's fondness for the construction of palaces, and Scorpio to their function as the guardians of temples. Lastly water, which appears in four medallions, evokes the palace's original natural setting, the island of the Te.

Underneath the tondi runs a motif of gilded garlands with ribbons that link up with the corbels of the ceiling, transformed into small stucco hermae representing satyrs. There is another, bizarre and fanciful, stucco frieze with representations of harpies and leonine protomes. The fireplace bears the inscription "F. Gonzaga II M. M. V SS. R. E. C. G." (Federicus Gonzaga II Marchio Mantuae V Sanctissimae Romanae Ecclesiae Capitanus Generalis) and the device of the salamander with its motto "Quod huic deest me torquet."

As far as the division of labor is concerned, this is the most recent opinion: Anselmo Guazzi was responsible for ten compartments (Diana, Venus, Mercury, and Jupiter, March, April, May, August, October, and November); Girolamo da Treviso for nine compartments (Minerva, Neptune, Apollo, Mars, Ceres, Juno, June, July, and September); Agostino da Mozzanega was paid for January and December; and Benedetto Pagni executed February.

The tondi on the south wall (Serpentarius, eagle, whale, ship and dolphin, goat), the bull on the west wall, and Arcturus setting on the east wall are attributed to Agostino.

80

Anselmo Guazzi painted the hare and the donkey under the influence of Mars on the west wall, and the waggoner and palace guardians (Arcturus rising) on the east wall. The tondi on the north wall are the work of Rinaldo. But Sirius (the lion hunt) may have been painted by Giulio himself. The hermae, festoons, and cornice are the work of Niccolò da Milano, while the decorations on the ceiling are by Andrea de' Conti.

In the decoration of the ceiling—in contrast to the previous "Sala di Psiche"—all effects of illusory depth and of foreshortening are avoided: the figures of the divinities and the months are set on the flat ground of the lozenges like elegant cameos. The scenes of earthly activities depicted in the tondi have animated backgrounds filled with charming scenery that are well suited to the extraordinary refinement of the figures on the ceiling.

Camera delle Aquile

Work was carried out on the "Camera delle Aquile," once Federico's bedchamber, and the wardrobe on the mezzanine above, from 1527 to 1528. According to the payments, Niccolò da Milano and Andrea de' Conti were responsible for the stuccos, and Agostino da Mozzanega for the paintings. The hypothesis has been put forward, on the basis of a letter dated 27 September 1527 in which Jacopo Calandra informs the marchese about the progress of the work and mentions "the Bolognese," that Primaticcio was also part of the *équipe* that worked on this room. If so, he may have been responsible for the frieze with putti in a vineyard and the ceiling panels, also in stucco, that represent divine loves.

It is worth pointing out the continual variation in the systems used for the ceilings of the rooms in the Palazzo Te: in the Chamber of the Eagles Giulio Romano, brilliant in his handling of structures and surfaces, succeeds in fusing walls and ceiling.

In the center of the ceiling is set an octagon, in which is depicted, with a daring use of foreshortening, the *Fall of Phaethon*. The corners of the room are transformed into four shells of gilded stucco, against which stand four heraldic eagles, taken from the

82

Gonzaga coat of arms.
Between the shells are set four lunettes, flanked by harpies, the traditional enemies of the eagles, standing on consoles. The lunettes, divided up into six rectangles by fascias of stucco, contain representations of divinities and cupids playing with attributes of the same divinities. Between the shells and four sides of the central octagon are arranged four stucco bas-reliefs that represent abductions carried out by the gods: the *Rape of Europa*, the *Rape of Proserpine*, the *Rape of Amphitrite*, and *Amymone Saved by Neptune*.
Just as the gods are subject to passions, so are the men, animals, and composite creatures similar to man that can be seen locked in combat in the frieze depicting the *Struggles of the Greeks against the Amazons*, the *Lapithae against the Centaurs*, and the *Nereids against the Tritons and Sea Monsters*.
Representation of the world of passions is well suited to the function of the room, used by Federico Gonzaga as his bedroom. But the scene of the *Fall of Phaethon* at the center of the ceiling looks like a warning not to fly too high, not to overstep the bounds. The *Fall of Phaethon* has also been interpreted as an allusion to the territory governed by the Gonzaga, for Phaethon, at the end of his flight, fell into the river Eridanus.

The following artists may have been responsible for the decoration: Primaticcio for the scenes in stucco of the divine abductions and the frieze with putti picking grapes, Niccolò da Milano for the decorations with figures, and Andrea de' Conti for the ornamental parts. The four friezes painted with figures can be ascribed as follows: the sea monsters on the south wall to Agostino da Mozzanega; the war with the Amazons on the west wall to Rinaldo; and the Centauromachia on the north wall, as well as the struggle amongst the animals above the east window, to Giulio. The scenes in the niches may have been painted by Anselmo Guazzi and Girolamo da Pontremoli. Identification of the author of the *Fall of Phaethon* remains open to question.

The frieze contains panoplies in stucco and three busts of Roman empresses (Aricidia, wife of Titus; Julia, wife of Septimus Severus; Julia Paula, wife of Heliogabalus) that are probably ancient sculptures, promised to Federico in 1527.

The use of classical materials in a modern setting is typical of Giulio Romano, whose ideas, as Pietro Aretino observed, were "anciently modern and modernly ancient." It should not be forgotten that in Giulio Romano's house in Mantua (still in existence)—of an unaccustomed magnificence appropriate only for an artist who was the true minister of the arts to his lord—there was a collection of Roman sculptures and coins, including part of the collection of Giovanni Ciampolini that Giulio had bought in Rome in 1520.

In Mantua Giulio Romano had access to the antiquities in the Gonzaga collection and shared his interest in ancient art with Federico Gonzaga, to whom he gave a number of pieces from his own collection. Stress should be laid on the extraordinary refinement—both of the marble and its carvings—of the fireplace in this room. It is inscribed with the motto "Quod huic deest me torquet" and Federico's initials, "F.G.II.M.M.V." The initials of the lord of Mantua also appear on the door that connects the "Camera delle Aquile" with the "Loggia di Davide."

Appartamento del Giardino Segreto
To keep the thematic coherence of the decorations intact, we shall now move on to the apartment—on the far side of the fishponds and the garden—referred to in contemporary documents as the "Appartamento del Giardino Segreto," and later known

as the "Appartamento della Grotta." As has been recently demonstrated, the grotto cannot be ascribed to Giulio Romano, but was created at the end of the sixteenth century on the basis of Tuscan models.

The decoration of the apartment was carried out from 1531 to 1534, with Andrea and Biagio de' Conti responsible for the stuccos and Luca da Faenza, Girolamo da Pontremoli, Benedetto Pagni, and Rinaldo Mantovano for the paintings.

The rooms made up a small apartment for the private meditations of Federico Gonzaga, comparable in size to the rooms used by Isabella d'Este in the Corte Vecchia of the Ducal Palace of Mantua. One enters through a vestibule with an octagonal plan, whose vault is decorated with grotesques. In fact it is one of the most refined and airy examples of this type of decoration.

As is well known, this decorative genre, which takes its inspiration from Nero's *Domus aurea*, was revived in Rome as a result of the fascination of Raphael's circle with archeological discoveries and was used in the Logge Vaticane, Villa Madama, Villa Lante, and the Farnesina. It involves a fantastic interlacery of plant forms mixed up with human figures and real and fanciful animals. In the vestibule of the apartment of the "Secret Garden," which is one of the earliest examples of grotesque decoration in northern Italy, the central octagon of the vault is transformed into a pergola: putti pick bunches of grapes and offer them to wild animals, while other beasts can be seen amidst stylized groups of trees. In the eight trapezoidal surfaces that link the octagon to the walls a web of plant forms extends over a light-colored ground, against which are set winged putti pouring liquids, masks, baskets of fruit, satyrs, and the Gonzaga device of Mount Olympus, which represents a mountain with a path winding up it. Girolamo da Pontremoli may have been the executor of the refined grotesque ornamentation.

Saletta di Attilio Regolo
The next room is the "Saletta di Attilio Regolo" (Small Room of Atilius Regulus), a small room with a quadrangular vault that again has an octagon at the center. Here the virtues of Federico Gonzaga are represented

83

Appartamento del Giardino Segreto, the Birth of Memnon.

Appartamento del Giardino Segreto, Work in the Fields.

allegorically, including the promotion of war, peace, science, and art.

Around this are set historical representations of famous men of the ancient world: Seleucus, accompanied by Justice; Cincinnatus, linked with Charity; Horace Coclites associated with Fortitude and Atilius Regulus with Prudence. In this case the decoration glorifies, through comparisons with illustrious men, the virtues of the lord. During these years, this same theme was to become a dominant one in the other rooms of the Palazzo Te as well, commencing with the "Loggia di Davide."

The decoration of the small loggia that opens onto the secret garden marks a return to the genre of the grotesque, which is well-suited to the rustic use of the apartment. The decoration, in which paintings and stuccos are harmoniously blended, extends over the barrel vault and the walls.

The eleven small scenes laid out as a narrative, and set in very fine frames with stuccos molded into cameos, can be interpreted as an allegory of man's life, stretching from birth to the ascension of the soul. However the scenes at the center of the vault—in one panel a young soul is carried to heaven; in a second two youths stand beside an old man, one pointing up and the other down, with an attending spirit leading one dark putto and one light one and with Diana in heaven; a third panel contains allegories of good and bad reputation—are still enigmatic and their literary source a mystery. One clue to their interpretation may be provided by a sixteenth century engraving by Giorgio Ghisi, depicting the episode of birth under the title of *Birth of Memnon*. Memnon was the mythical son of Tithonus and Eos (Aurora), and the king of Ethiopia. His legend was widely-known in the Hellenistic and Egyptian worlds.

The fresco in the middle of the long wall of the loggia depicts the *Marriage of Peleus and Thetis*. The grotesques in this loggia achieve a happy balance between naturalistic and caricatural elements and erudite citations. The former include very lively satyrs and animals running wild amidst the interlacery of vegetation, as well as the lunette depicting *Rest in the Fields*, which is indicative of a fresh interest in rural life on the part of Giulio Romano. The scenes were painted by Anselmo Guazzi and Agostino da Mozzanega.

The citations of antiquity include the scene showing *Silenus on a Biga,* or two-horse chariot, which has been identified as a copy of the subject of a Bacchic relief, probably Roman from the Augustan period, that is now in the "Sala dei Capitani" (Captains' Room) of the Ducal Palace in Mantua but which was originally set, along with another relief of a Dionysiac subject, in the sides of a window in the eastern wall of the "Loggia dei Marmi" (Loggia of Marbles) in the "Appartamento di Troia" (Apartment of Troy) in the same building. We know this from a drawing made by Andreasino in 1568 and now in the Kunstmuseum in Düsseldorf. In the "Loggia dei Marmi," on which he was to work from 1534 to 1539, Giulio Romano provided a setting in an antique style of architecture for the Gonzaga collection of marbles, busts, and reliefs, some of them classical and some from the Renaissance.

The walls of the secret garden were frescoed, as can be seen from a few surviving traces, with architectural perspectives representing an open gallery with spiral columns and fountains. Giulio Romano intended to create an illusory opening in the walls of the *hortus conclusus* by means of a trick of perspective that extended the enclosed space of the garden. The graffito traces are easier to reconstruct with the aid of a sixteenth century sketch: this is a folio from the so-called *Mantuan Album* (Berlin, Staatliche Museen) of Martin van Heemskerk, a significant collection of drawings of Roman and Mantuan subjects made by a northern European artist in the early decades of the century.

If we consider that the side door of the small loggia, now walled up, originally led outside, then we can see that the observer was presented with two views of the countryside, one real and the other imaginary.

Giulio Romano showed a preference for spiral or Solomonic columns, previously used by Raphael in the cartoon for the tapestry of *Peter Healing the Cripple.* In his Roman works (Sala di Costantino in the Vatican, the *Circumcision of Christ* now in the Louvre), Giulio Romano had already created architectural scenes with spiral columns. They are also to be found in the decorations of the "Sala di Psiche" in the Palazzo Te, in the scene of *Venus, Mars, and Adonis.*

Spiral columns dominate the facade of the Rustica, one of Giulio Romano's most original architectural creations, built on the grounds of the Ducal Palace.

But let us return to the Secret Garden. In the fascia of the attic, studded with hermae, there are niches on three sides containing representations of Aesop's Fables. Originally there were eighteen of them, but only ten survive today: eight in stucco and two frescos. The stuccos were probably executed by Niccolò da Milano and Andrea de' Conti.

The subjects of the remaining fables are as follows: the puppy, the master, and the donkey; the lion and the mouse; the fox and the crow; the fox and the stork; the horse and the lion; the fly and the bald man; the dog that carried a piece of meat in its mouth; the wolf and the sculpted head; the lion and the shepherd; and the shepherd and the wolf.

It has been suggested that the representations are based on the Veronese edition of Aesop's Fables (*Aesopus moralisatus* of 1479, illustrated with woodcuts, of which the marchese of Mantua, Federico I Gonzaga (1441-1484), possessed a copy. It should not be forgotten that around the same time the theme was also used in the decoration of the *Magna Domus* of Cardinal Bernardo Cles in Trent.

In the middle of the wall of the loggia a sepulchral monument for a dog is represented: it has been suggested that it may refer to a bitch owned by Federico II, which died in 1526 while giving birth. To commemorate the animal—"which we would like to have buried in a fine marble tomb" as Federico wrote to Giulio Romano in a letter dated 15 October 1526—the prince asked for two designs from his artist.

The Gonzagas' fondness for dogs has been pointed out on many occasions. It had an influence on the iconography in Mantegna's *Camera picta* as well, and a clear symbolic significance, connected with the virtue of faithfulness.

Portico with spiral columns, anonymous drawing inspired by the decorations of the court of the Appartamento Segreto. Berlin, Kupferstichkabinett.

Court of the Appartamento del Giardino Segreto.

*Court of the Appartamento del Giardino
Segreto, detail.*

90

The grotto, which is set beyond the door surrounded by rocky concretions, remains to be described. It has already been explained that it is not the work of Giulio Romano, but was constructed in the late sixteenth century on the lines of grottos created in Tuscany. Its decoration dates from the first few decades of the seventeenth century: the device outlined on the floor in pebbles with the motto "Non mutuata luce" belongs to the period of Ferdinando Gonzaga (1612-1626). The frescos, which depict mysterious mythical episodes connected with the sea, painted in the upper part of the grotto as openings between encrustations of many different materials, suggest the work of a painter who collaborated with Antonio Maria Viani in the early part of the century.

After 1530 the themes of the decorations in the palace altered in relation to shifts in the position of the Gonzaga dynasty.
During these years the Gonzaga seigniory moved definitively into the political orbit of the Habsburgs and the Spanish. After the Peace of Cambrai, the European scene was dominated by Charles V, who presented himself to the Italian princes as the founder of the *renovatio imperii*, which would restore Astraea, that is Justice.
In August 1529 the marchese of Mantua went to Genoa to pay homage to Charles V, who had just arrived in Italy. The title of captain general of the imperial army in Italy was bestowed on Federico. The marchese of Mantua hoped to succeed the Sforza in the Duchy of Milan, but his expectations were frustrated by the actions of Pope Clement VII. Federico realized that the only hope of territorial expansion lay in the emperor.
In the spring of 1530 Charles V, recently raised to emperor in Bologna, paid a visit to Mantua. Fine displays were set up during his stay, triumphal arches in the classical style that are described in detail in the *Cronaca del Soggiorno di Carlo V in Italia*, attributed to a member of the Gonzaga family, Luigi, who was an eyewitness to these celebrations.
The imperial progress, which concluded in the cathedral square where a very tall column had been set up with a Victory at its

Loggia di Davide, David Decapitates Goliah.

top, was lined with decorations for which Giulio Romano had supplied the designs.

On this occasion Federico Gonzaga was invested with the title of duke by the emperor, to whose policies he was then bound by a strengthened tie of loyalty.

Significant new decorations also resulted from Federico's marriage to Margherita Paleologo, celebrated at Casale Monferrato on 3 October 1531: this ensured the continuance of the house of Gonzaga and the investiture of the Monferrato, which was to be made definitive in 1536.

For the occasion of the duke's marriage, Giulio Romano was distracted from his work on the Palazzo Te by the commission to build a small palace for the bride, close to the moat of the Castle by the bridge of San Giorgio. This construction was destroyed at the end of the last century. Giulio Romano set all his collaborators to work not only on the new building, but also on an apartment for Margherita on the piano nobile of the Castle. In 1532 Charles V paid his second visit to Mantua. Once again temporary decorations and spectacles were prepared for his arrival.

To solemnize the entry of the emperor, Giulio Romano had Fermo da Caravaggio paint "various life-size figures with various spoils and trophies and frames" on the facade of the Palazzo Te overlooking the fishponds. These decorations have now vanished.

The intention of celebrating imperial authority was not limited to the creation of temporary displays, but also shaped the iconographic program of the new apartment. The amorous and hedonistic myths connected with *otium* disappeared and the salamander, emblem of the torments of love, was no longer to be seen.

Olympian myths, triumphs in the ancient manner, allegories of virtues, and glorifications of classical heroes furnished the images for the rooms that follow the "Loggia di Davide." The presence of Charles V transformed the Palazzo Te, in origin a residence for "honest idleness," into an imperial palace.

Federico, with the help of Giulio Romano, liked to present the image of a warrior prince. Thus he surrounded himself with

Camera degli Stucchi.

Camera degli Stucchi, detail with the central lunette.

portrayals of illustrious commanders and an allegorical repertory that drew on the monuments of the past. The recourse to the classical aura and the use of erudite citations offered security and authority. The new ideological content—the use of art as *instrumentum regni* is significant in this case—found expression in Giulio Romano's work in a more austere language, with touches of purism and an abandonment of the playful and comic tone that had characterized much of the earlier decorations in the palace.

Loggia di Davide

The eastern loggia was decorated from 1531 to 1534. The work was carried out with dispatch in order to have the loggia ready for the entrance of Charles V in November 1532. For this occasion the scaffolding was removed, as it was in the "Sala dei Giganti," in order to show the decorations to the emperor. The paintings were soon in need of restoration, carried out in 1533-1534 by Luca da Faenza.

The scenes depicting *David and Bathsheba, Bathsheba Bathing,* and *David and Goliath* with two putti are attributed to Rinaldo Mantovano; the one of *David and Uriah* to Benedetto Pagni. In the fall of 1532 Fermo da Caravaggio painted three lunettes on the west wall—*David Fighting the Bear, David Fighting the Lion,* and the Gonzaga coat of arms—and collaborated on the lunette on the south wall representing *David Playing the Harp.*

The stucco moldings of the vault are the work of Recanato and the de' Conti brothers, Biagio and Andrea. They are also thought to be responsible for the medallions on the ceiling representing scenes from the life of David. The ornamentation of plants and foliage is the work of Benedetto Bertoldo.

A series of letters written in 1530 informs us that it was the intention of Federico and Giulio to obtain statues of famous leaders to be located in the loggia. The theme of the man of arms was especially popular at the

Sala dei Giganti, details.

courts, where the *jus imaginum* helped to legitimate power, embodying the *virtus* of the military commander in exemplary figures. Nor should it be forgotten that Paolo Giovio, in his own villa at Borgovico near Como, presented these images in cycles devoted to different sets of men of arms and of letters.

The statues for the "Loggia di Davide," commissioned from Alfonso Cittadella, were not executed. The statues that now occupy the niches of the loggia are of mysterious origin. Nicodemo Tessin, in his account of a journey made in 1688, claims them to be the work of a sculpture named Niccini. Niccini can be identified as the Bolognese sculptor Francesco Agnesini, whose presence in the Palazzo Te is documented from 1653-1654. Agnesini, together with another Bolognese sculptor Gabriele Brunelli, worked on the construction of a fountain in the palace gardens, which has now vanished.

The stuccos in the loggia, simulating bronze reliefs and representing scenes from the life of David, are the work of Giovanni Bellavite, a modeler employed by Paolo Pozzo during the restorations he carried out in 1809.

Federico Gonzaga identified himself with the biblical king David: in fact the scenes are depictions of strength, amorous abandonment, or poetic inspiration that refer specifically to the personality of the lord of Mantua. There is an allusion to events at the Mantuan court in the episode where David kills Uriah, the husband of Bathsheba. The biblical story has parallels with a crime committed by Federico Gonzaga when he had Francesco Gonzaga da Calvisano, the husband of his lover Isabella Boschetti, put to death after accusing him of taking part in a plot.

Sala degli Stucchi

The theme of decorations of the "Sala degli Stucchi" is also a martial one, linked with the revival of antiquity. The barrel vault is divided up into twenty-five coffers depicting small scenes of historical and mythological inspiration. At the center of the vault are the three Fates that preside over the course of human life.

Hercules and Mars are depicted in the lunettes, again in stucco, surrounded by a sunburst of panels with representations of Victories.

A line of soldiers is represented in the double frieze, based on the reliefs of Roman columns. There are various historical interpretations of the parade: an inscription in the room, no longer visible today, used to read "Federici auspiciis ducis invicti et optimi / hic est videre ut incedebant copiae / romanae nostrum quod diu latuit saeculum."

The procession of soldiers is described by Strada as "how the Romans used to go to war." An engraving by Pietro Santi Bartoli identifies, in the text written by Bellori, the line of soldiers as the triumphal entry of Emperor Sigismund into Mantua in 1433. It was he who conferred the title of marquis on Gianfrancesco Gonzaga.

More recent interpretations have seen it as representing Charles V's entry into Mantua: in this view the two-headed Eagle on the shield of one of the soldiers would allude to Charles V. This hypothesis is founded on the preparatory drawing of a victory in which the name "Carol," alluding to the emperor, is written on a shield. However it is the prevailing view today that the folio in the Uffizi does not necessarily represent a design for the victories in the eastern lunette, but a study for the decoration of a triumphal arch.

The most convincing interpretation of the military parade is that it is a generic triumph in the ancient manner.

The closest reference for the procession remains that of the reliefs on ancient Roman columns, reinforced by the influence of Mantegna's *Triumphs of Caesar*. The famous series of the *Triumphs of Caesar*, made up of nine tempera paintings sold by the Gonzagas to the English royal family in 1627 and now on show at Hampton Court, was hung in the Palazzo di San Sebastiano, not far from the Palazzo Te. The figures, as in a bas-relief, are arranged in a procession: they are one of the finest evocations of the classical world and a perfect expression of the passion for antiquity that Mantegna felt so strongly.

In the second edition of the *Lives* (1568), Vasari claims that Primaticcio and Giovan Battista Scultori worked on the Room of the Stuccos. The participation of the former,

who moved to France in 1531, is highly controversial. More recent investigations tend to limit Primaticcio's intervention, on stylistic bases, to the lunette representing Mars, where one can recognize the delicate elegance that the artist was to demonstrate at Fontainebleau.

In the absence of documents, the stuccos of the procession and those of the coffers in the ceiling, less refined than the ones in the lunettes, can be ascribed to the de' Conti brothers.

The decoration adheres in a restrained fashion to the background, from which stand out episodes in practical frames, with a balanced subdivision of areas. The three-dimensional projection is confined to a limited number of planes and makes no attempt at illusionistic effects.

Camera dell'Imperatore or di Cesare

Caesar is also the subject of the next room, known as the "Camera dell'Imperatore" or "di Cesare." No documents relating to this decoration have been found and its authors have been identified on the basis of stylistic differences: the style of Fermo da Caravaggio has been recognized in the central panel; that of Rinaldo Mantovano in the Augustus on the west wall, the four emperors alongside the tondi, and the *Continence of Scipio*. The panel depicting Alexander the Great on the west wall and the tondo with *Alexander and the Books of Homer* have been attributed to Giulio himself.

The frieze that runs beneath the ceiling, representing putti, was executed by the academic Mantuan painter Felice Campi during the restorations carried out in the late eighteenth century.

Let us return to the iconographic program: *Caesar Having the Letters of Pompey Burned* is depicted in an octagonal area at the center of the ceiling. From the octagon depart six rectangular panels depicting emperors, of which five can be identified: Caesar, Philip of Macedon, Alexander, and Augustus.

On the long sides of the room, two tondi illustrate the *Continence of Scipio* and *Alexander Discovering the Books of Homer*. The ceiling, decorated with geometric interlacery subjected to alterations in the neoclassical era, also bears the devices of Federico Gonzaga: Cupid between two trees, Mount Olympus, and the salamander.

Through the reference to classical examples, the decoration alludes to the virtues of sovereigns, such as generosity, respect for people's rights, and patronage of the arts and culture.

Sala dei Giganti

From here one enters the "Sala dei Giganti," one of the most astounding features of the palace and always recalled with wonder in the descriptions made by travelers in the past.

There is ample documentation of the decoration of this room. Rinaldo Mantovano worked on it from 1 March 1531 till 31 July 1534, with a break in November 1532 on the occasion of Charles V's visit to Mantua. At that time the ceiling area must have been already complete: the scaffolding was drawn away to allow the emperor to admire the unusual composition.

Between 5 March and 30 September 1532 Fermo da Caravaggio executed the temple in the middle of the vault; between April and July 1534 he painted landscapes and rocks, with the assistance of Luca da Faenza. The east-facing wall of the fireplace and the south wall date from the period between 1532 and August 1534. Rinaldo may have worked on the two remaining walls up until 1534-1536.

As far as the theme is concerned, it is worth taking another look at the admiring comments of Giorgio Vasari. On a visit to Mantua in 1541, the historian from Arezzo was taken round the palace by Giulio Romano and has left us a detailed description of the "Sala dei Giganti" that is filled with emotional intensity. It is worth quoting some passages from it: "[...] for Giulio, who was most original and ingenious, to show what he was worth, in a corner of the palace that was similar to the aforementioned room of Psyche, set out to make a room, whose walls would be the same as a painting, to deceive as far as possible the men who would see it. Thus having built this corner, which was on a marshy site, with deep and double foundations, he had erected over the corner a large round room

Sala dei Giganti, detail.

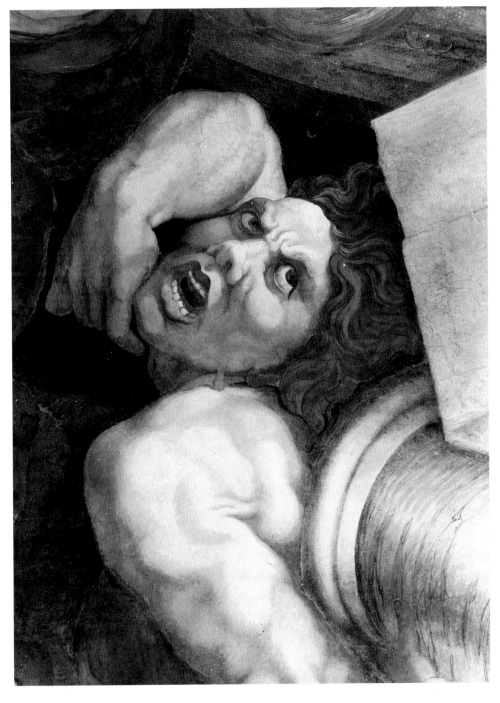

100

with very thick walls, in order that the four corners of that wall should look more robust from the outer part and would be able to support a double and round vault in the manner of an oven: and this done, having that chamber corners, for the rounding of that to its places he had the doors, windows, and fireplace built with roughly rounded stones, and almost in a disjointed and wrong way, that seemed to lean in one side, and to really be falling down: and with that room walled up so strangely, he set to painting the most original invention that could be found, that is Jupiter crushing the Giants."

The throne of Jupiter is depicted in heaven inside a temple on a central plan. Lower down is an enraged Jupiter striking the Giants with thunderbolts, assisted by Juno. The Winds blow toward the earth while the goddess Ops turns with her lions at the sound of the thunderbolts. The gods of Olympus—among whom we can recognize Venus, Mars, and Mommus with open arms—are struck with horror. Even the Graces and the Horae are filled with terror. The Moon departs with Saturn and Janus, as do Neptune and Minerva with the nine Muses. Pan embraces a nymph as if to save her. Apollo remains on the chariot of the Sun, which is held back by the Horae. Surrounded by satyrs and nymphs, Bacchus and Silenus cannot hide their fear and Vulcan looks toward Hercules, who is speaking with Mercury. Alongside Mercury stand Vertumnus and Pomona. Below them are the Giants. But let us return to Vasari's description: "[...] and in this place is set, between these crumbling walls, the fireplace of the room, which shows, when the fire is lit, that the giants are burning [...] and thus Giulio with this understanding of the fire taken from the story, makes a beautiful ornament to the fireplace.

"In this work Giulio, to make it more frightening and terrible, also had the great giants of strange stature (being in different ways struck by the lightning and bolts) fall to earth, and some are in front and some behind, some dead, some wounded, and some covered by mountains and ruins of buildings. Wherefore no one thought ever to see work of brush more horrible and

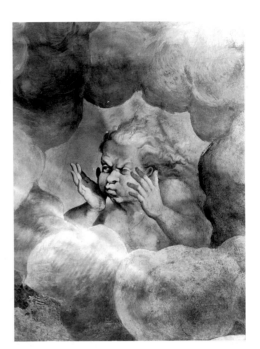

102

frightening or more natural than this; and whoever enters in that room, seeing the windows, doors, and other such things twisted, and as if about to collapse, and the mountains, and the buildings falling, cannot but fear that everything will crash down upon him, seeing especially in that heaven all the Gods rushing here and there in flight: and that which is marvelous in this work, is seeing that all that painting has no beginning nor end, and all attached and so well joined together, without boundary or division of ornament, so that the things that are close to the buildings appear very large, and those that are far off, where there are villages, are lost in infinity; wherefore that room, which is no longer than fifteen ells, looks like a stretch of countryside with villages; without which, the floor being of small round stones set on edge, and the beginning of the walls that run straight painted with the same stones, there appears to be no sharp corner, and that plane comes

to look like a very great thing; which was done with much discretion and great art by Giulio, to whom our artificers owe much for such inventions."

Vasari's account, sensitive to the unusual spatial quality of the room, not only provides us with clues to the identification of the mythical figures, but with a description of the effect of the now vanished fireplace and the original flooring of stones. These elements were removed by the architect Paolo Pozzo during the restoration of the palace. Between 1784 and 1785 Paolo Pozzo furnished designs for the floor of the room. What was eventually realized was the great circle with concentric patterns that can be seen today. This accentuates the dynamism of the composition, but reveals the junction between floor and walls and therefore impairs the spatial continuity that Giulio Romano had achieved and that so impressed Vasari.

The original appearance of the room was

Sala dei Giganti, detail.

104   also altered by the loss of the fireplace, removed at the end of the eighteenth century as it had blackened the walls and allowed damp to enter. Previously the fireplace had provided both the visual effect of moving flames and the sound effect of crackling.

The literary sources for the myth of the Giants are Hesiod's *Theogony*, the *Fasti*, and above all the first book of Ovid's *Metamorphoses*. It is not unlikely that Giulio Romano consulted a learned humanist when drawing up the program for his representation of the myth.

The myth of Jupiter crushing the Giants is rich in symbolic significance. The political interpretation of the myth is widely accepted: Jupiter is identified with Emperor Charles V, while the defeated giants symbolize the Italian princes who rebelled against the Empire.

The "Sala dei Giganti" serves as the antechamber to the racquets court in which Charles V played with courtiers during his 1530 visit. Consequently the posture of Jupiter as he hurls the thunderbolt has been seen as a transfiguration of the emperor's gesture as he launches the ball. Other elements of the decoration are open to ambivalent interpretations: Mount Olympus, the thunderbolt, and the eagle are all attributes of Jupiter, but they are also devices of the Gonzaga. Finally Jupiter hurling thunderbolts is a symbol of the imperial power which the Gonzaga saw as the source of their own fortune.

It should not be forgotten that other decorations carried out during the same period in connection with the visit of Charles V can be interpreted as celebrations and eulogies of the emperor. An example of this is the fresco of the *Fall of the Giants* in Palazzo Doria at Fassolo (Genoa), painted by Perin del Vaga. It is a fact that in August 1529, while decorations were being prepared for Charles V's entry into Genoa, Federico Gonzaga went to the Ligurian city to pay homage to the emperor.

A theme similar to that of the Giants must have been used for the triumphal displays created to Giulio Romano's designs for Charles V's entry into Milan in August 1541. One element in the ceremonial route, described in A. Albicante's *Trattato dell'intrar in Milano di Carlo V* (1541), was a four-faced arch in the Piazza del Duomo, surmounted by an equestrian statue of the emperor. Beneath the horse stood three giants symbolizing the emperor's expedition to Africa in order to protect Europe from the depredations of the corsairs, the defense of Christianity from the Turkish advance, and the conquest of America.

There is also one of Charles V's medals dating from around 1549, designed by Leone Leoni and probably connected with the battle of Mühlberg, with a representation of Jupiter striking the Giants with lightning on the reverse, an allegorical celebration of the emperor's victory over the Protestants.

It has already been pointed out that Giulio Romano drew on the *Metamorphoses* of Ovid, which were available to him in contemporary translations into the vulgar tongue and included commentaries and embellishments of an allegorical and moralizing nature.

On the basis of these texts (the translation by Nicolò degli Agostini, Venice 1522; the one by Giovanni de' Bonsignori which was printed five times in Venice and Milan between 1497 and 1522), it is possible to make further identifications.

The dreadful figures over the fireplace (east wall) are Giants and not Cyclopes. The figure with horses and a two-pronged fork is Pluto, on whose right are the Furies, infernal creatures with snakes instead of hair. The giant spitting fire above the fireplace is Typhoeus, again the protagonist of one of Ovid's myths, who presumed to grow as tall as heaven. Jupiter imprisoned the giant beneath the island of Sicily, who struggled against this with all his might, making the earth tremble and creating the volcano of Etna. The outlines of the giant's body suggest the triangular shape of Sicily, while Typhoeus's head marks the position of Etna. The original fireplace must have created the illusion that the giant was surrounded by flames.

Small monkeys wander through the rocks of the hideous landscape, splashed with blood. This detail, which has no parallel in Ovid's tale, finds an explanation in the aforementioned commentaries by Agostini and Bonsi-

Sala dei Giganti, detail with the vault.

gnori. The monkeys, which medieval culture regarded as diabolical creatures and a degeneration of the human race, were generated out of the blood of the giants.

On the wall to the left of the entrance to the room there is the following inscription: "Quaenam spes hominum post praelia Phlegrae" (What hope for men after the rash assault on Phlegra?). These words (Statius, *Thebaid*, X, v. 909) are spoken by Jupiter before destroying Capaneus, whose legend can be compared to that of the Giants, and they take on the significance of a religious admonishment.

The monkeys symbolize the proud who consider themselves superior to God. Thus the rebellion against the emperor is also a sin against religion, for imperial power defends the Christian faith and is the image of God on earth.

In the realization of the "Sala dei Giganti," Giulio Romano took to an extreme his natural penchant for caprice and license, which has already been pointed out in other parts of the palace's architecture and decorations. In the "Sala dei Giganti" form renounces its spatial limits and approaches the dimension of scenography. All the elements are unleashed in a setting dominated by the impression of an enclosed vortex, whose distressing effect is not the result solely of the monstrous images painted on the surfaces of the walls and ceiling, which the glow of the fire must have rendered still more disquieting, but also of the threatening mass of the false cupola. The ceiling appears to project the sacred zone of heaven onto earth and assail the spectator from above, giving him the feeling that he is about to be crushed by the collapsing structure.

Another effect of the room, always mentioned in the accounts of travelers in the past, is the echo, which permits words whispered in one corner of the room to be heard in the opposite corner. This acoustic

artifice, a trick typical of the courts, interacts with the visual impressions to create something that approaches total theater. The terrible effect of the room lies in the way an enclosed space has been manipulated so that it creates the overall impression of matter in rebellion.

This results in an unhinging of the architecturally elaborated forms, such as the Serlian arch of the temple of the Giants, the column that breaks, and the stones of the fireplace that regress to the formless stage of the rustic style. The painting, in which artifice and illusion are taken to extremes, triumphs over and negates all stylized elements.

There is a marked contrast between the upper and lower parts of the "Sala dei Giganti." The vault is transformed illusionistically into a cupola that recalls the one designed by Raphael for the Chigi chapel in Santa Maria del Popolo in Rome, as well as Bramante's small temple of San Pietro in Montorio, again in Rome. In his bold use of foreshortening, Giulio Romano also reminds us of the oculus painted by Mantegna at the center of the vault of the *Camera picta* in Mantua castle.

In the lower part the representation of the twisted forms of the Giants falling from buildings and mountains is marked by a furious jumble of bodies, but also by agitated expressions and exaggerated gestures. It should not be forgotten that in 1506, while Giulio Romano was still a boy, the extraordinary discovery of the group of the *Laocoön* was made in Rome (Giulio Romano was to recall it in the "Sala di Troia" of Federico Gonzaga's apartment in the Ducal Palace in Mantua). This was regarded by connoisseurs and artists as one of the highest expressions of ancient art because of its plastic vitality and intensity of expression. In some of the Giants' heads, representing pain and anguish, Giulio Romano seems to be citing the famous Hellenistic marble sculpture, taken as a paragon of dynamic tension.

Between the seventeenth and eighteenth century the "Sala dei Giganti" underwent considerable degradation: during the wars that marked the period stretching from the Sack of Mantua (1630) to the war of Polish succession (1733-1735), Mantua became a bivouac for troops. Even the Palazzo Te was used to quarter the soldiers, who often left graffiti on the walls, writing their own names, many of them foreign, and the date. During the recent restoration (1988) it was decided to leave the numerous graffiti in the lower section of the room as a historical testimony. These graffiti were not covered over, but directly reintegrated by glazing the plaster.

Rooms in the South Wing

The rooms in the south wing have generally been neglected on tours of the palace. These rooms, together with a number of other undecorated ones on the west side that are connected with the corner room used as a kitchen, were originally reserved for the palace's domestic staff. At the end of the eighteenth century and the beginning of the nineteenth, the lower part of the walls was embellished with stuccos and new plastering.

In the immediate vicinity of the "Sala dei Giganti" there are three small rooms for whose decoration payments were made, between October 1533 and November 1534, to the stuccoworkers Andrea and Biagio de' Conti and Benedetto Bertoldo, known as Il Pretino, and to the painters Girolamo da Pontremoli and Luca da Faenza. The room on the courtyard side has a square plan and has grotesque decorations on the ceiling and stuccos in the lunettes. Next to it is a room known as the "Camerino delle Grottesche" (Small Room of the Grotesques), with an octagonal vault supported by elegant and slender painted columns with lion's heads in stucco. In the four corners of the room are ram's heads modeled in stucco. The tiny passageway has a circular medallion on its ceiling, surrounded by grotesques, containing the figure of Venus.

After these rooms, in which there is a return to grotesque decoration in the manner of Raphael, there are rooms on which Niccolò da Milano, Giovan Battista Scultori, Andrea de' Conti, and Agostino da Mozzanega were working as early as 1527-1528. In the first, known as the "Camera dei Candelabri," there are a number of candelabra and seven tondi attributed to Niccolò, while the gro-

tesque armed figures in the corners are the work of Agostino. The same painters worked on the next room, known as the "Camera delle Cariatidi" (Chamber of the Caryatids): it is probably to this that a payment made to Agostino da Mozzanega in 1528 for the decoration of a grotesque frieze refers. The stuccos of the lower frieze—symbolizing the parts of the day—come from the "Loggia dei Marmi" of the "Appartamento di Troia" in the Ducal Palace in Mantua and were moved here in 1813. Giulio's preparatory designs for the unusual figures of caryatids and satyrs have survived.

Beyond the southern loggia is the "Camera delle Vittorie" (Chamber of Victories), for which a payment was made in favor of Nic-

colò da Milano. The Victories, modeled in stucco, emphasize the corners of the room. There is an unusual decoration in the wooden coffers of the ceiling with motifs of women looking out of windows, combing their hair, and picking out lice. The ceiling seems to be in a different style to that of Giulio Romano and more in keeping with the Mantuan tradition that refers, in its iconography as well, to the tondo of Mantegna's *Camera picta* and the room known as the "Sala della Scalcheria" (Room of the Carver) decorated by Leombruno in Isabella's apartment in the Ducal Palace. The artist may have been a certain Lupino, pupil of Lorenzo Costa, who was working on the Palazzo Te in 1538.

Bibliography

L.B. Alberti, *De re aedificatoria* (Italian trans. *L'architettura*, edited by G. Orlandi and P. Portoghesi, Milan 1966), 1450.

G. Vasari, *Le vite de' più eccellenti Architetti, Pittori, et Scultori italiani, da Cimabue insino a' tempi nostri*, Florence 1550.

G. Vasari, *Le vite de' più eccellenti Pittori, Scultori et Architetti*, Florence 1568 (edited by G. Milanesi, vol. V, Florence 1880).

P. Giovio, *Dialogo delle imprese militari et amorose*, Lyons 1574.

A. Ulloa, *Vita dell'invittissimo e sacratissimo Imperator Carlo Quinto*, Venice 1574.

G. Cadioli, *Descrizione delle pitture, sculture ed architetture che si osservano nella città di Mantova e ne' suoi contorni*, Mantua 1763.

L.C. Volta, *Descrizione storica delle pitture del regio ducale Palazzo del Te*, Mantua 1783.

C. D'Arco, *Istoria della vita e delle opere di Giulio Pippi Romano*, Mantua (2nd revised and expanded ed., Mantua 1842), Mantua 1838.

A. Luzio, "Federico Gonzaga ostaggio alla corte di Giulio II," in *Archivio della R. Società Romana di Storia Patria*, IX, 1886, pp. 509-582.

G. Romano, *Cronaca del soggiorno di Carlo V in Italia*, Milan 1892.

P. Carpi, "Giulio Romano ai servigi di Federico II Gonzaga," in *Atti e Mem. della R. Acc. Virgiliana*, nos. 11-13, 1920, pp. 35-152.

E. Gombrich, "Zum Werke Giulio Romanos," in *Jahrbuch der Kunsthistorischen Sammlungen in Wien*, n.s., VIII, 1934, pp. 79-104; IX, pp. 121-150 (Italian trans. in *Quaderni di Palazzo Te*, 1984, I, pp. 23-79).

E. Gombrich, "The Sala dei Venti in the Palazzo del Te," in *Journal of the Warburg and Courtauld Institutes*, XXX, 1950, pp. 121-150.

F. Hartt, "Gonzaga Symbols in the Palazzo del Te," in *Journal of the Warburg and Courtauld Institutes*, XXX, 1950, pp. 151-188.

G. Paccagnini, *Il Palazzo Te*, Milan 1957.

F. Hartt, *Giulio Romano*, New Haven 1958.

E. Marani, C. Perina, *Mantova: le Arti*, II, Mantua 1961.

E. Verheyen, "Correggio's 'Amori di Giove,'" in *Journal of the Warburg and Courtauld Institutes*, 29, 1966, pp. 160-192.

J. Shearman, "Giulio Romano, tradizione, licenze, artifici," in *Bollettino del C.I.S.A. "Andrea Palladio,"* IX, 1967, pp. 354-368.

J. Shearman, "Osservazioni sulla cronologia e l'evoluzione del Palazzo Te," in *Bollettino del C.I.S.A. "Andrea Palladio,"* IX, 1967, pp. 434-438.

E. Verheyen, "Jacopo Strada's Mantuan Drawings of 1567-1568," in *The Art Bulletin*, XLIX, 1967, pp. 62-69.

M. Tafuri, "Il mito naturalistico nell'architettura del '500," in *L'Arte*, I, n.s., 1968, pp. 7-36.

E. Verheyen, "Die Sala di Ovidio im Palazzo del Te," in *Römische Jahrbuch für Kunstgeschichte*, 12, 1969, pp. 61-170.

K.W. Forster, R.J. Tuttle, "The Palazzo del Te," in *Journal of the Society of Architectural Historians*, XXX, 4, 1971, pp. 267-293.

E. Verheyen, "Die Malerei in der Sala di Psiche des Palazzo del Te," in *Jahrbuch der Berliner Museen*, 1972, pp. 363-368.

A. Belluzzi, W. Capezzali, *Il palazzo dei lucidi inganni. Palazzo Te a Mantova*, Florence 1976.

B. Guthmuller, "Ovidiibersetzungen und mythologische Malerei Bemerkungen zur Sala dei Giganti Giulio Romano," in *Mitteilungen des Kunsthistorischen Inst. in Florenz*, XXI, I, 1977, pp. 35-68.

E. Verheyen, *The Palazzo del Te in Mantua, Images of Love and Politics*, Baltimore and London 1977.

E. Gombrich, "Hypnerotomachiana, III, Giulio Romano e Sebastiano del Piombo," in *Immagini simboliche*, Turin 1978.

R. Signorini, "Distat enim quae sydera te excipiant," in *Journal of the Warburg and Courtauld Institutes*, XLII, 1979, p. 273.

A. Belluzzi, "Carlo V a Mantova e a Milano," in Var. Authors, *La città effimera e l'universo artificiale del giardino*, Rome 1980, pp. 47-62.

M. Praz in Var. Authors, *Splendours of the Gonzaga* (Cat. of the London exhibition), Milan 1981.

B. Allies, "Palazzo del Te. Order, Orthodoxy and the Orders," in *Architectural Review*, 5, 1983, pp. 59-65.

R. Signorini, *La "Fabella" di Psiche e altra mitologia*, Mantua 1983.

D. Nicolini, *La corte rurale nel Mantovano*, Milan 1984.

D. Arasse, "Giulio Romano e il labirinto di Psiche," in *Quaderni di Palazzo Te*, 3, 1985, pp. 7-18.

M. Azzi Visentini, "Nicolò Sebregondi," in *Il Seicento nell'arte e nella cultura* (proceedings of the convention held in Mantua in 1983), Milan 1985, pp. 103-111.

114 S. Borsi, *Giuliano da Sangallo – I disegni di architettura e dell'antico*, Rome 1985.

D. Lenzi, "Dal Seghizzi al Monti ai Bibiena – Architetti e scenografi bolognesi a Mantova sotto gli ultimi Gonzaga," in *Il Seicento nell'arte e nella cultura* (proceedings of the convention held in Mantua in 1983), Milan 1985, pp. 164-173.

R. Signorini, "Postilla a Psiche," in *Quaderni del Palazzo Te*, 3, 1985, pp. 27-28.

A. Bruschi, "Baldassare Peruzzi nel Palazzo di Francesco Fusconi da Norcia," in *Architettura – storia e documenti*, 2, 1986, pp. 11-30.

A. Belluzzi, "La grotta di Palazzo Te a Mantova," in *Atti del Convegno "Per la conoscenza e la conservazione delle grotte artificiali,"* Genoa 1987, pp. 49-57.

P. Carpeggiani, C. Tellini Perina, *Giulio Romano a Mantova*, Mantua 1987.

G. Erbesato, *Il Palazzo Te di Giulio Romano*, Florence 1987.

L. Guerrini, "Due rilievi antichi nel Palazzo Ducale di Mantova e un dipinto di Palazzo Te," in *Quaderni di Palazzo Te*, 7, 1987, pp. 35-43.

R. Signorini, "Le favole di Esopo nel 'giardino segreto' della Villa del Te," in *Quaderni di Palazzo Te*, 8, 1988, pp. 21-36.

C. Belfanti, C. Tellini Perina, G. Basile, *I Giganti di Palazzo Te*, Mantua 1989.

Var. Authors, *Giulio Romano*, catalogue of the exhibition in Mantua, Milan 1989.

Var. Authors, *Pittura a Mantova dal Romanico al Settecento*, ed. by C. Tellini Perina, Milan 1989.

A. Belluzzi, K.W. Forster, in Var. Authors, *Giulio Romano*, catalogue of the exhibition in Mantua, Milan 1989.

G. Suitner, in Var. Authors, *Pittura a Mantova dal Romanico al Settecento*, ed. by. C. Tellini Perina, Milan 1989.

M. Tafuri, in Var. Authors, *Giulio Romano*, catalogue of the exhibition in Mantua, Milan 1989.

U. Bazzotti, *Le imprese di Palazzo Te* (report given to the convention on Giulio Romano, Mantua, October 1989), to be published in 1990.

Printed for Electa by
Fantonigrafica - Elemond Editori Associati